CW01647219

For God

January 1

Our wonderful Father in Heaven, we bring to You ALL of Your children who were born on January the 1st and we ask for Your blessings in their lives. We ask that they would know Your love and care as well as Your great plans for them. We ask for You to provide for them and their families, for You to put love and forgiveness in their hearts and for You to keep them safe. We give each one of them to You and agree for Your Divine blessing over them, their family and the community where they reside, in Jesus' name we pray, together.

Amen.

Loved Ones' Birth Days or Other Requests

____

____

____

____

January 2

Our wonderful Father in Heaven, we bring to You ALL of Your children who were born on January the 2nd and we ask for Your blessings in their lives. We ask that they would know Your love and care as well as Your great plans for them. We ask for You to provide for them and their families, for You to put love and forgiveness in their hearts and for You to keep them safe. We give each one of them to You and agree for Your Divine blessing over them, their family and the community where they reside, in Jesus' name we pray, together.

Amen.

Loved Ones' Birth Days or Other Requests

____

____

____

____

January 3

Our wonderful Father in Heaven, we bring to You ALL of Your children who were born on January the 3rd and we ask for Your blessings in their lives. We ask that they would know Your love and care as well as Your great plans for them. We ask for You to provide for them and their families, for You to put love and forgiveness in their hearts and for You to keep them safe. We give each one of them to You and agree for Your Divine blessing over them, their family and the community where they reside, in Jesus' name we pray, together.

Amen.

Loved Ones' Birth Days or Other Requests

____

____

____

____

January 4

Our wonderful Father in Heaven, we bring to You ALL of Your children who were born on January the 4th and we ask for Your blessings in their lives. We ask that they would know Your love and care as well as Your great plans for them. We ask for You to provide for them and their families, for You to put love and forgiveness in their hearts and for You to keep them safe. We give each one of them to You and agree for Your Divine blessing over them, their family and the community where they reside, in Jesus' name we pray, together.
Amen.

Loved Ones' Birth Days or Other Requests

____

____

____

____

January 5

Our wonderful Father in Heaven, we bring to You ALL of Your children who were born on January the 5th and we ask for Your blessings in their lives. We ask that they would know Your love and care as well as Your great plans for them. We ask for You to provide for them and their families, for You to put love and forgiveness in their hearts and for You to keep them safe. We give each one of them to You and agree for Your Divine blessing over them, their family and the community where they reside, in Jesus' name we pray, together.
Amen.

Loved Ones' Birth Days or Other Requests

____

____

____

____

January 6

Our wonderful Father in Heaven, we bring to You ALL of Your children who were born on January the 6th and we ask for Your blessings in their lives. We ask that they would know Your love and care as well as Your great plans for them. We ask for You to provide for them and their families, for You to put love and forgiveness in their hearts and for You to keep them safe. We give each one of them to You and agree for Your Divine blessing over them, their family and the community where they reside, in Jesus' name we pray, together.

Amen.

Loved Ones' Birth Days or Other Requests

____

____

____

____

January 7

Our wonderful Father in Heaven, we bring to You ALL of Your children who were born on January the 7th and we ask for Your blessings in their lives. We ask that they would know Your love and care as well as Your great plans for them. We ask for You to provide for them and their families, for You to put love and forgiveness in their hearts and for You to keep them safe. We give each one of them to You and agree for Your Divine blessing over them, their family and the community where they reside, in Jesus' name we pray, together.

Amen.

Loved Ones' Birth Days or Other Requests

____

____

____

____

January 8

Our wonderful Father in Heaven, we bring to You ALL of Your children who were born on January the 8th and we ask for Your blessings in their lives. We ask that they would know Your love and care as well as Your great plans for them. We ask for You to provide for them and their families, for You to put love and forgiveness in their hearts and for You to keep them safe. We give each one of them to You and agree for Your Divine blessing over them, their family and the community where they reside, in Jesus' name we pray, together.
Amen.

Loved Ones' Birth Days or Other Requests

____

____

____

____

January 9

Our wonderful Father in Heaven, we bring to You ALL of Your children who were born on January the 9th and we ask for Your blessings in their lives. We ask that they would know Your love and care as well as Your great plans for them. We ask for You to provide for them and their families, for You to put love and forgiveness in their hearts and for You to keep them safe. We give each one of them to You and agree for Your Divine blessing over them, their family and the community where they reside, in Jesus' name we pray, together.
Amen.

Loved Ones' Birth Days or Other Requests

____

____

____

____

January 10

Our wonderful Father in Heaven, we bring to You ALL of Your children who were born on January the 10th and we ask for Your blessings in their lives. We ask that they would know Your love and care as well as Your great plans for them. We ask for You to provide for them and their families, for You to put love and forgiveness in their hearts and for You to keep them safe. We give each one of them to You and agree for Your Divine blessing over them, their family and the community where they reside, in Jesus' name we pray, together.

Amen.

Loved Ones' Birth Days or Other Requests

____

____

____

____

January 11

Our wonderful Father in Heaven, we bring to You ALL of Your children who were born on January the 11th and we ask for Your blessings in their lives. We ask that they would know Your love and care as well as Your great plans for them. We ask for You to provide for them and their families, for You to put love and forgiveness in their hearts and for You to keep them safe. We give each one of them to You and agree for Your Divine blessing over them, their family and the community where they reside, in Jesus' name we pray, together.

Amen.

Loved Ones' Birth Days or Other Requests

____

____

____

____

January 12

Our wonderful Father in Heaven, we bring to You ALL of Your children who were born on January the 12th and we ask for Your blessings in their lives. We ask that they would know Your love and care as well as Your great plans for them. We ask for You to provide for them and their families, for You to put love and forgiveness in their hearts and for You to keep them safe. We give each one of them to You and agree for Your Divine blessing over them, their family and the community where they reside, in Jesus' name we pray, together.
Amen.

Loved Ones' Birth Days or Other Requests

____

____

____

____

January 13

Our wonderful Father in Heaven, we bring to You ALL of Your children who were born on January the 13th and we ask for Your blessings in their lives. We ask that they would know Your love and care as well as Your great plans for them. We ask for You to provide for them and their families, for You to put love and forgiveness in their hearts and for You to keep them safe. We give each one of them to You and agree for Your Divine blessing over them, their family and the community where they reside, in Jesus' name we pray, together.
Amen.

Loved Ones' Birth Days or Other Requests

____

____

____

____

January 14

Our wonderful Father in Heaven, we bring to You ALL of Your children who were born on January the 14th and we ask for Your blessings in their lives. We ask that they would know Your love and care as well as Your great plans for them. We ask for You to provide for them and their families, for You to put love and forgiveness in their hearts and for You to keep them safe. We give each one of them to You and agree for Your Divine blessing over them, their family and the community where they reside, in Jesus' name we pray, together.

Amen.

Loved Ones' Birth Days or Other Requests

____

____

____

____

January 15

Our wonderful Father in Heaven, we bring to You ALL of Your children who were born on January the 15th and we ask for Your blessings in their lives. We ask that they would know Your love and care as well as Your great plans for them. We ask for You to provide for them and their families, for You to put love and forgiveness in their hearts and for You to keep them safe. We give each one of them to You and agree for Your Divine blessing over them, their family and the community where they reside, in Jesus' name we pray, together.

Amen.

Loved Ones' Birth Days or Other Requests

____

____

____

____

January 16

Our wonderful Father in Heaven, we bring to You ALL of Your children who were born on January the 16th and we ask for Your blessings in their lives. We ask that they would know Your love and care as well as Your great plans for them. We ask for You to provide for them and their families, for You to put love and forgiveness in their hearts and for You to keep them safe. We give each one of them to You and agree for Your Divine blessing over them, their family and the community where they reside, in Jesus' name we pray, together.

Amen.

Loved Ones' Birth Days or Other Requests

____

____

____

____

January 17

Our wonderful Father in Heaven, we bring to You ALL of Your children who were born on January the 17th and we ask for Your blessings in their lives. We ask that they would know Your love and care as well as Your great plans for them. We ask for You to provide for them and their families, for You to put love and forgiveness in their hearts and for You to keep them safe. We give each one of them to You and agree for Your Divine blessing over them, their family and the community where they reside, in Jesus' name we pray, together.
Amen.

Loved Ones' Birth Days or Other Requests

____

____

____

____

January 18

Our wonderful Father in Heaven, we bring to You ALL of Your children who were born on January the 18th and we ask for Your blessings in their lives. We ask that they would know Your love and care as well as Your great plans for them. We ask for You to provide for them and their families, for You to put love and forgiveness in their hearts and for You to keep them safe. We give each one of them to You and agree for Your Divine blessing over them, their family and the community where they reside, in Jesus' name we pray, together.

Amen.

Loved Ones' Birth Days or Other Requests

____

____

____

____

January 19

Our wonderful Father in Heaven, we bring to You ALL of Your children who were born on January the 19th and we ask for Your blessings in their lives. We ask that they would know Your love and care as well as Your great plans for them. We ask for You to provide for them and their families, for You to put love and forgiveness in their hearts and for You to keep them safe. We give each one of them to You and agree for Your Divine blessing over them, their family and the community where they reside, in Jesus' name we pray, together.

Amen.

Loved Ones' Birth Days or Other Requests

____

____

____

____

January 20

Our wonderful Father in Heaven, we bring to You ALL of Your children who were born on January the 20th and we ask for Your blessings in their lives. We ask that they would know Your love and care as well as Your great plans for them. We ask for You to provide for them and their families, for You to put love and forgiveness in their hearts and for You to keep them safe. We give each one of them to You and agree for Your Divine blessing over them, their family and the community where they reside, in Jesus' name we pray, together.

Amen.

Loved Ones' Birth Days or Other Requests

____

____

____

____

January 21

Our wonderful Father in Heaven, we bring to You ALL of Your children who were born on January the 21st and we ask for Your blessings in their lives. We ask that they would know Your love and care as well as Your great plans for them. We ask for You to provide for them and their families, for You to put love and forgiveness in their hearts and for You to keep them safe. We give each one of them to You and agree for Your Divine blessing over them, their family and the community where they reside, in Jesus' name we pray, together.

Amen.

Loved Ones' Birth Days or Other Requests

____

____

____

____

January 22

Our wonderful Father in Heaven, we bring to You ALL of Your children who were born on January the 22nd and we ask for Your blessings in their lives. We ask that they would know Your love and care as well as Your great plans for them. We ask for You to provide for them and their families, for You to put love and forgiveness in their hearts and for You to keep them safe. We give each one of them to You and agree for Your Divine blessing over them, their family and the community where they reside, in Jesus' name we pray, together.

Amen.

Loved Ones' Birth Days or Other Requests

____

____

____

____

January 23

Our wonderful Father in Heaven, we bring to You ALL of Your children who were born on January the 23rd and we ask for Your blessings in their lives. We ask that they would know Your love and care as well as Your great plans for them. We ask for You to provide for them and their families, for You to put love and forgiveness in their hearts and for You to keep them safe. We give each one of them to You and agree for Your Divine blessing over them, their family and the community where they reside, in Jesus' name we pray, together.
Amen.

Loved Ones' Birth Days or Other Requests

____

____

____

____

January 24

Our wonderful Father in Heaven, we bring to You ALL of Your children who were born on January the 24th and we ask for Your blessings in their lives. We ask that they would know Your love and care as well as Your great plans for them. We ask for You to provide for them and their families, for You to put love and forgiveness in their hearts and for You to keep them safe. We give each one of them to You and agree for Your Divine blessing over them, their family and the community where they reside, in Jesus' name we pray, together.

Amen.

Loved Ones' Birth Days or Other Requests

____

____

____

____

January 25

Our wonderful Father in Heaven, we bring to You ALL of Your children who were born on January the 25th and we ask for Your blessings in their lives. We ask that they would know Your love and care as well as Your great plans for them. We ask for You to provide for them and their families, for You to put love and forgiveness in their hearts and for You to keep them safe. We give each one of them to You and agree for Your Divine blessing over them, their family and the community where they reside, in Jesus' name we pray, together.
Amen.

Loved Ones' Birth Days or Other Requests

____

____

____

____

January 26

Our wonderful Father in Heaven, we bring to You ALL of Your children who were born on January the 26th and we ask for Your blessings in their lives. We ask that they would know Your love and care as well as Your great plans for them. We ask for You to provide for them and their families, for You to put love and forgiveness in their hearts and for You to keep them safe. We give each one of them to You and agree for Your Divine blessing over them, their family and the community where they reside, in Jesus' name we pray, together.

Amen.

Loved Ones' Birth Days or Other Requests

____

____

____

____

January 27

Our wonderful Father in Heaven, we bring to You ALL of Your children who were born on January the 27th and we ask for Your blessings in their lives. We ask that they would know Your love and care as well as Your great plans for them. We ask for You to provide for them and their families, for You to put love and forgiveness in their hearts and for You to keep them safe. We give each one of them to You and agree for Your Divine blessing over them, their family and the community where they reside, in Jesus' name we pray, together.
Amen.

Loved Ones' Birth Days or Other Requests

____

____

____

____

January 28

Our wonderful Father in Heaven, we bring to You ALL of Your children who were born on January the 28th and we ask for Your blessings in their lives. We ask that they would know Your love and care as well as Your great plans for them. We ask for You to provide for them and their families, for You to put love and forgiveness in their hearts and for You to keep them safe. We give each one of them to You and agree for Your Divine blessing over them, their family and the community where they reside, in Jesus' name we pray, together.

Amen.

Loved Ones' Birth Days or Other Requests

____

____

____

____

January 29

Our wonderful Father in Heaven, we bring to You ALL of Your children who were born on January the 29th and we ask for Your blessings in their lives. We ask that they would know Your love and care as well as Your great plans for them. We ask for You to provide for them and their families, for You to put love and forgiveness in their hearts and for You to keep them safe. We give each one of them to You and agree for Your Divine blessing over them, their family and the community where they reside, in Jesus' name we pray, together.
Amen.

Loved Ones' Birth Days or Other Requests

____

____

____

____

January 30

Our wonderful Father in Heaven, we bring to You ALL of Your children who were born on January the 30th and we ask for Your blessings in their lives. We ask that they would know Your love and care as well as Your great plans for them. We ask for You to provide for them and their families, for You to put love and forgiveness in their hearts and for You to keep them safe. We give each one of them to You and agree for Your Divine blessing over them, their family and the community where they reside, in Jesus' name we pray, together.

Amen.

Loved Ones' Birth Days or Other Requests

____

____

____

____

January 31

Our wonderful Father in Heaven, we bring to You ALL of Your children who were born on January the 31st and we ask for Your blessings in their lives. We ask that they would know Your love and care as well as Your great plans for them. We ask for You to provide for them and their families, for You to put love and forgiveness in their hearts and for You to keep them safe. We give each one of them to You and agree for Your Divine blessing over them, their family and the community where they reside, in Jesus' name we pray, together.

Amen.

Loved Ones' Birth Days or Other Requests

____

____

____

____

February 1

Our wonderful Father in Heaven, we bring to You ALL of Your children who were born on February the 1st and we ask for Your blessings in their lives. We ask that they would know Your love and care as well as Your great plans for them. We ask for You to provide for them and their families, for You to put love and forgiveness in their hearts and for You to keep them safe. We give each one of them to You and agree for Your Divine blessing over them, their family and the community where they reside, in Jesus' name we pray, together.
Amen.

Loved Ones' Birth Days or Other Requests

____

____

____

____

February 2

Our wonderful Father in Heaven, we bring to You ALL of Your children who were born on February the 2nd and we ask for Your blessings in their lives. We ask that they would know Your love and care as well as Your great plans for them. We ask for You to provide for them and their families, for You to put love and forgiveness in their hearts and for You to keep them safe. We give each one of them to You and agree for Your Divine blessing over them, their family and the community where they reside, in Jesus' name we pray, together.
Amen.

Loved Ones' Birth Days or Other Requests

____

____

____

____

February 3

Our wonderful Father in Heaven, we bring to You ALL of Your children who were born on February the 3rd and we ask for Your blessings in their lives. We ask that they would know Your love and care as well as Your great plans for them. We ask for You to provide for them and their families, for You to put love and forgiveness in their hearts and for You to keep them safe. We give each one of them to You and agree for Your Divine blessing over them, their family and the community where they reside, in Jesus' name we pray, together.

Amen.

Loved Ones' Birth Days or Other Requests

____

____

____

____

February 4

Our wonderful Father in Heaven, we bring to You ALL of Your children who were born on February the 4th and we ask for Your blessings in their lives. We ask that they would know Your love and care as well as Your great plans for them. We ask for You to provide for them and their families, for You to put love and forgiveness in their hearts and for You to keep them safe. We give each one of them to You and agree for Your Divine blessing over them, their family and the community where they reside, in Jesus' name we pray, together.

Amen.

Loved Ones' Birth Days or Other Requests

____

____

____

____

February 5

Our wonderful Father in Heaven, we bring to You ALL of Your children who were born on February the 5th and we ask for Your blessings in their lives. We ask that they would know Your love and care as well as Your great plans for them. We ask for You to provide for them and their families, for You to put love and forgiveness in their hearts and for You to keep them safe. We give each one of them to You and agree for Your Divine blessing over them, their family and the community where they reside, in Jesus' name we pray, together.
Amen.

Loved Ones' Birth Days or Other Requests

____

____

____

____

February 6

Our wonderful Father in Heaven, we bring to You ALL of Your children who were born on February the 6th and we ask for Your blessings in their lives. We ask that they would know Your love and care as well as Your great plans for them. We ask for You to provide for them and their families, for You to put love and forgiveness in their hearts and for You to keep them safe. We give each one of them to You and agree for Your Divine blessing over them, their family and the community where they reside, in Jesus' name we pray, together.
Amen.

Loved Ones' Birth Days or Other Requests

____

____

____

____

February 7

Our wonderful Father in Heaven, we bring to You ALL of Your children who were born on February the 7th and we ask for Your blessings in their lives. We ask that they would know Your love and care as well as Your great plans for them. We ask for You to provide for them and their families, for You to put love and forgiveness in their hearts and for You to keep them safe. We give each one of them to You and agree for Your Divine blessing over them, their family and the community where they reside, in Jesus' name we pray, together.
Amen.

Loved Ones' Birth Days or Other Requests

____

____

____

____

February 8

Our wonderful Father in Heaven, we bring to You ALL of Your children who were born on February the 8th and we ask for Your blessings in their lives. We ask that they would know Your love and care as well as Your great plans for them. We ask for You to provide for them and their families, for You to put love and forgiveness in their hearts and for You to keep them safe. We give each one of them to You and agree for Your Divine blessing over them, their family and the community where they reside, in Jesus' name we pray, together.

Amen.

Loved Ones' Birth Days or Other Requests

____

____

____

____

February 9

Our wonderful Father in Heaven, we bring to You ALL of Your children who were born on February the 9th and we ask for Your blessings in their lives. We ask that they would know Your love and care as well as Your great plans for them. We ask for You to provide for them and their families, for You to put love and forgiveness in their hearts and for You to keep them safe. We give each one of them to You and agree for Your Divine blessing over them, their family and the community where they reside, in Jesus' name we pray, together.

Amen.

Loved Ones' Birth Days or Other Requests

____

____

____

____

February 10

Our wonderful Father in Heaven, we bring to You ALL of Your children who were born on February the 10th and we ask for Your blessings in their lives. We ask that they would know Your love and care as well as Your great plans for them. We ask for You to provide for them and their families, for You to put love and forgiveness in their hearts and for You to keep them safe. We give each one of them to You and agree for Your Divine blessing over them, their family and the community where they reside, in Jesus' name we pray, together.

Amen.

Loved Ones' Birth Days or Other Requests

____

____

____

____

February 11

Our wonderful Father in Heaven, we bring to You ALL of Your children who were born on February the 11th and we ask for Your blessings in their lives. We ask that they would know Your love and care as well as Your great plans for them. We ask for You to provide for them and their families, for You to put love and forgiveness in their hearts and for You to keep them safe. We give each one of them to You and agree for Your Divine blessing over them, their family and the community where they reside, in Jesus' name we pray, together.

Amen.

Loved Ones' Birth Days or Other Requests

____

____

____

____

February 12

Our wonderful Father in Heaven, we bring to You ALL of Your children who were born on February the 12th and we ask for Your blessings in their lives. We ask that they would know Your love and care as well as Your great plans for them. We ask for You to provide for them and their families, for You to put love and forgiveness in their hearts and for You to keep them safe. We give each one of them to You and agree for Your Divine blessing over them, their family and the community where they reside, in Jesus' name we pray, together.

Amen.

Loved Ones' Birth Days or Other Requests

____

____

____

____

February 13

Our wonderful Father in Heaven, we bring to You ALL of Your children who were born on February the 13th and we ask for Your blessings in their lives. We ask that they would know Your love and care as well as Your great plans for them. We ask for You to provide for them and their families, for You to put love and forgiveness in their hearts and for You to keep them safe. We give each one of them to You and agree for Your Divine blessing over them, their family and the community where they reside, in Jesus' name we pray, together.

Amen.

Loved Ones' Birth Days or Other Requests

____

____

____

____

February 14

Our wonderful Father in Heaven, we bring to You ALL of Your children who were born on February the 14th and we ask for Your blessings in their lives. We ask that they would know Your love and care as well as Your great plans for them. We ask for You to provide for them and their families, for You to put love and forgiveness in their hearts and for You to keep them safe. We give each one of them to You and agree for Your Divine blessing over them, their family and the community where they reside, in Jesus' name we pray, together.
Amen.

Loved Ones' Birth Days or Other Requests

____

____

____

____

February 15

Our wonderful Father in Heaven, we bring to You ALL of Your children who were born on February the 15th and we ask for Your blessings in their lives. We ask that they would know Your love and care as well as Your great plans for them. We ask for You to provide for them and their families, for You to put love and forgiveness in their hearts and for You to keep them safe. We give each one of them to You and agree for Your Divine blessing over them, their family and the community where they reside, in Jesus' name we pray, together.
Amen.

Loved Ones' Birth Days or Other Requests

____

____

____

____

February 16

Our wonderful Father in Heaven, we bring to You ALL of Your children who were born on February the 16th and we ask for Your blessings in their lives. We ask that they would know Your love and care as well as Your great plans for them. We ask for You to provide for them and their families, for You to put love and forgiveness in their hearts and for You to keep them safe. We give each one of them to You and agree for Your Divine blessing over them, their family and the community where they reside, in Jesus' name we pray, together.
Amen.

Loved Ones' Birth Days or Other Requests

____

____

____

____

February 17

Our wonderful Father in Heaven, we bring to You ALL of Your children who were born on February the 17th and we ask for Your blessings in their lives. We ask that they would know Your love and care as well as Your great plans for them. We ask for You to provide for them and their families, for You to put love and forgiveness in their hearts and for You to keep them safe. We give each one of them to You and agree for Your Divine blessing over them, their family and the community where they reside, in Jesus' name we pray, together.
Amen.

Loved Ones' Birth Days or Other Requests

____

____

____

____

February 18

Our wonderful Father in Heaven, we bring to You ALL of Your children who were born on February the 18th and we ask for Your blessings in their lives. We ask that they would know Your love and care as well as Your great plans for them. We ask for You to provide for them and their families, for You to put love and forgiveness in their hearts and for You to keep them safe. We give each one of them to You and agree for Your Divine blessing over them, their family and the community where they reside, in Jesus' name we pray, together.

Amen.

Loved Ones' Birth Days or Other Requests

____

____

____

____

February 19

Our wonderful Father in Heaven, we bring to You ALL of Your children who were born on February the 19th and we ask for Your blessings in their lives. We ask that they would know Your love and care as well as Your great plans for them. We ask for You to provide for them and their families, for You to put love and forgiveness in their hearts and for You to keep them safe. We give each one of them to You and agree for Your Divine blessing over them, their family and the community where they reside, in Jesus' name we pray, together.

Amen.

Loved Ones' Birth Days or Other Requests

____

____

____

____

February 20

Our wonderful Father in Heaven, we bring to You ALL of Your children who were born on February the 20th and we ask for Your blessings in their lives. We ask that they would know Your love and care as well as Your great plans for them. We ask for You to provide for them and their families, for You to put love and forgiveness in their hearts and for You to keep them safe. We give each one of them to You and agree for Your Divine blessing over them, their family and the community where they reside, in Jesus' name we pray, together.

Amen.

Loved Ones' Birth Days or Other Requests

____

____

____

____

February 21

Our wonderful Father in Heaven, we bring to You ALL of Your children who were born on February the 21st and we ask for Your blessings in their lives. We ask that they would know Your love and care as well as Your great plans for them. We ask for You to provide for them and their families, for You to put love and forgiveness in their hearts and for You to keep them safe. We give each one of them to You and agree for Your Divine blessing over them, their family and the community where they reside, in Jesus' name we pray, together.

Amen.

Loved Ones' Birth Days or Other Requests

____

____

____

____

February 22

Our wonderful Father in Heaven, we bring to You ALL of Your children who were born on February the 22nd and we ask for Your blessings in their lives. We ask that they would know Your love and care as well as Your great plans for them. We ask for You to provide for them and their families, for You to put love and forgiveness in their hearts and for You to keep them safe. We give each one of them to You and agree for Your Divine blessing over them, their family and the community where they reside, in Jesus' name we pray, together.

Amen.

Loved Ones' Birth Days or Other Requests

____

____

____

____

February 23

Our wonderful Father in Heaven, we bring to You ALL of Your children who were born on February the 23rd and we ask for Your blessings in their lives. We ask that they would know Your love and care as well as Your great plans for them. We ask for You to provide for them and their families, for You to put love and forgiveness in their hearts and for You to keep them safe. We give each one of them to You and agree for Your Divine blessing over them, their family and the community where they reside, in Jesus' name we pray, together.

Amen.

Loved Ones' Birth Days or Other Requests

____

____

____

____

February 24

Our wonderful Father in Heaven, we bring to You ALL of Your children who were born on February the 24th and we ask for Your blessings in their lives. We ask that they would know Your love and care as well as Your great plans for them. We ask for You to provide for them and their families, for You to put love and forgiveness in their hearts and for You to keep them safe. We give each one of them to You and agree for Your Divine blessing over them, their family and the community where they reside, in Jesus' name we pray, together.

Amen.

Loved Ones' Birth Days or Other Requests

____

____

____

____

February 25

Our wonderful Father in Heaven, we bring to You ALL of Your children who were born on February the 25th and we ask for Your blessings in their lives. We ask that they would know Your love and care as well as Your great plans for them. We ask for You to provide for them and their families, for You to put love and forgiveness in their hearts and for You to keep them safe. We give each one of them to You and agree for Your Divine blessing over them, their family and the community where they reside, in Jesus' name we pray, together.

Amen.

Loved Ones' Birth Days or Other Requests

____

____

____

____

February 26

Our wonderful Father in Heaven, we bring to You ALL of Your children who were born on February the 26th and we ask for Your blessings in their lives. We ask that they would know Your love and care as well as Your great plans for them. We ask for You to provide for them and their families, for You to put love and forgiveness in their hearts and for You to keep them safe. We give each one of them to You and agree for Your Divine blessing over them, their family and the community where they reside, in Jesus' name we pray, together.
Amen.

Loved Ones' Birth Days or Other Requests

____

____

____

____

February 27

Our wonderful Father in Heaven, we bring to You ALL of Your children who were born on February the 27th and we ask for Your blessings in their lives. We ask that they would know Your love and care as well as Your great plans for them. We ask for You to provide for them and their families, for You to put love and forgiveness in their hearts and for You to keep them safe. We give each one of them to You and agree for Your Divine blessing over them, their family and the community where they reside, in Jesus' name we pray, together.
Amen.

Loved Ones' Birth Days or Other Requests

____

____

____

____

February 28

Our wonderful Father in Heaven, we bring to You ALL of Your children who were born on February the 28th and we ask for Your blessings in their lives. We ask that they would know Your love and care as well as Your great plans for them. We ask for You to provide for them and their families, for You to put love and forgiveness in their hearts and for You to keep them safe. We give each one of them to You and agree for Your Divine blessing over them, their family and the community where they reside, in Jesus' name we pray, together.
Amen.

Loved Ones' Birth Days or Other Requests

____

____

____

____

February 29

Our wonderful Father in Heaven, we bring to You ALL of Your children who were born on February the 29th and we ask for Your blessings in their lives. We ask that they would know Your love and care as well as Your great plans for them. We ask for You to provide for them and their families, for You to put love and forgiveness in their hearts and for You to keep them safe. We give each one of them to You and agree for Your Divine blessing over them, their family and the community where they reside, in Jesus' name we pray, together.

Amen.

Loved Ones' Birth Days or Other Requests

____

____

____

____

March 1

Our wonderful Father in Heaven, we bring to You ALL of Your children who were born on March the 1st and we ask for Your blessings in their lives. We ask that they would know Your love and care as well as Your great plans for them. We ask for You to provide for them and their families, for You to put love and forgiveness in their hearts and for You to keep them safe. We give each one of them to You and agree for Your Divine blessing over them, their family and the community where they reside, in Jesus' name we pray, together.

Amen.

Loved Ones' Birth Days or Other Requests

____

____

____

____

March 2

Our wonderful Father in Heaven, we bring to You ALL of Your children who were born on March the 2nd and we ask for Your blessings in their lives. We ask that they would know Your love and care as well as Your great plans for them. We ask for You to provide for them and their families, for You to put love and forgiveness in their hearts and for You to keep them safe. We give each one of them to You and agree for Your Divine blessing over them, their family and the community where they reside, in Jesus' name we pray, together.

Amen.

Loved Ones' Birth Days or Other Requests

____

____

____

____

March 3

Our wonderful Father in Heaven, we bring to You ALL of Your children who were born on March the 3rd and we ask for Your blessings in their lives. We ask that they would know Your love and care as well as Your great plans for them. We ask for You to provide for them and their families, for You to put love and forgiveness in their hearts and for You to keep them safe. We give each one of them to You and agree for Your Divine blessing over them, their family and the community where they reside, in Jesus' name we pray, together.
Amen.

Loved Ones' Birth Days or Other Requests

____

____

____

____

March 4

Our wonderful Father in Heaven, we bring to You ALL of Your children who were born on March the 4th and we ask for Your blessings in their lives. We ask that they would know Your love and care as well as Your great plans for them. We ask for You to provide for them and their families, for You to put love and forgiveness in their hearts and for You to keep them safe. We give each one of them to You and agree for Your Divine blessing over them, their family and the community where they reside, in Jesus' name we pray, together.
Amen.

Loved Ones' Birth Days or Other Requests

____

____

____

____

March 5

Our wonderful Father in Heaven, we bring to You ALL of Your children who were born on March the 5th and we ask for Your blessings in their lives. We ask that they would know Your love and care as well as Your great plans for them. We ask for You to provide for them and their families, for You to put love and forgiveness in their hearts and for You to keep them safe. We give each one of them to You and agree for Your Divine blessing over them, their family and the community where they reside, in Jesus' name we pray, together.
Amen.

Loved Ones' Birth Days or Other Requests

____

____

____

____

March 6

Our wonderful Father in Heaven, we bring to You ALL of Your children who were born on March the 6th and we ask for Your blessings in their lives. We ask that they would know Your love and care as well as Your great plans for them. We ask for You to provide for them and their families, for You to put love and forgiveness in their hearts and for You to keep them safe. We give each one of them to You and agree for Your Divine blessing over them, their family and the community where they reside, in Jesus' name we pray, together.

Amen.

Loved Ones' Birth Days or Other Requests

____

____

____

____

March 7

Our wonderful Father in Heaven, we bring to You ALL of Your children who were born on March the 7th and we ask for Your blessings in their lives. We ask that they would know Your love and care as well as Your great plans for them. We ask for You to provide for them and their families, for You to put love and forgiveness in their hearts and for You to keep them safe. We give each one of them to You and agree for Your Divine blessing over them, their family and the community where they reside, in Jesus' name we pray, together.
Amen.

Loved Ones' Birth Days or Other Requests

____

____

____

____

March 8

Our wonderful Father in Heaven, we bring to You ALL of Your children who were born on March the 8th and we ask for Your blessings in their lives. We ask that they would know Your love and care as well as Your great plans for them. We ask for You to provide for them and their families, for You to put love and forgiveness in their hearts and for You to keep them safe. We give each one of them to You and agree for Your Divine blessing over them, their family and the community where they reside, in Jesus' name we pray, together.
Amen.

Loved Ones' Birth Days or Other Requests

____

____

____

____

March 9

Our wonderful Father in Heaven, we bring to You ALL of Your children who were born on March the 9th and we ask for Your blessings in their lives. We ask that they would know Your love and care as well as Your great plans for them. We ask for You to provide for them and their families, for You to put love and forgiveness in their hearts and for You to keep them safe. We give each one of them to You and agree for Your Divine blessing over them, their family and the community where they reside, in Jesus' name we pray, together.
Amen.

Loved Ones' Birth Days or Other Requests

____

____

____

____

March 10

Our wonderful Father in Heaven, we bring to You ALL of Your children who were born on March the 10th and we ask for Your blessings in their lives. We ask that they would know Your love and care as well as Your great plans for them. We ask for You to provide for them and their families, for You to put love and forgiveness in their hearts and for You to keep them safe. We give each one of them to You and agree for Your Divine blessing over them, their family and the community where they reside, in Jesus' name we pray, together.

Amen.

Loved Ones' Birth Days or Other Requests

____

____

____

____

March 11

Our wonderful Father in Heaven, we bring to You ALL of Your children who were born on March the 11th and we ask for Your blessings in their lives. We ask that they would know Your love and care as well as Your great plans for them. We ask for You to provide for them and their families, for You to put love and forgiveness in their hearts and for You to keep them safe. We give each one of them to You and agree for Your Divine blessing over them, their family and the community where they reside, in Jesus' name we pray, together.
Amen.

Loved Ones' Birth Days or Other Requests

____

____

____

____

March 12

Our wonderful Father in Heaven, we bring to You ALL of Your children who were born on March the 12th and we ask for Your blessings in their lives. We ask that they would know Your love and care as well as Your great plans for them. We ask for You to provide for them and their families, for You to put love and forgiveness in their hearts and for You to keep them safe. We give each one of them to You and agree for Your Divine blessing over them, their family and the community where they reside, in Jesus' name we pray, together.
Amen.

Loved Ones' Birth Days or Other Requests

____

____

____

____

March 13

Our wonderful Father in Heaven, we bring to You ALL of Your children who were born on March the 13th and we ask for Your blessings in their lives. We ask that they would know Your love and care as well as Your great plans for them. We ask for You to provide for them and their families, for You to put love and forgiveness in their hearts and for You to keep them safe. We give each one of them to You and agree for Your Divine blessing over them, their family and the community where they reside, in Jesus' name we pray, together.

Amen.

Loved Ones' Birth Days or Other Requests

____

____

____

____

March 14

Our wonderful Father in Heaven, we bring to You ALL of Your children who were born on March the 14th and we ask for Your blessings in their lives. We ask that they would know Your love and care as well as Your great plans for them. We ask for You to provide for them and their families, for You to put love and forgiveness in their hearts and for You to keep them safe. We give each one of them to You and agree for Your Divine blessing over them, their family and the community where they reside, in Jesus' name we pray, together.

Amen.

Loved Ones' Birth Days or Other Requests

____

____

____

____

March 15

Our wonderful Father in Heaven, we bring to You ALL of Your children who were born on March the 15th and we ask for Your blessings in their lives. We ask that they would know Your love and care as well as Your great plans for them. We ask for You to provide for them and their families, for You to put love and forgiveness in their hearts and for You to keep them safe. We give each one of them to You and agree for Your Divine blessing over them, their family and the community where they reside, in Jesus' name we pray, together.

Amen.

Loved Ones' Birth Days or Other Requests

____

____

____

____

March 16

Our wonderful Father in Heaven, we bring to You ALL of Your children who were born on March the 16th and we ask for Your blessings in their lives. We ask that they would know Your love and care as well as Your great plans for them. We ask for You to provide for them and their families, for You to put love and forgiveness in their hearts and for You to keep them safe. We give each one of them to You and agree for Your Divine blessing over them, their family and the community where they reside, in Jesus' name we pray, together.
Amen.

Loved Ones' Birth Days or Other Requests

____

____

____

____

March 17

Our wonderful Father in Heaven, we bring to You ALL of Your children who were born on March the 17th and we ask for Your blessings in their lives. We ask that they would know Your love and care as well as Your great plans for them. We ask for You to provide for them and their families, for You to put love and forgiveness in their hearts and for You to keep them safe. We give each one of them to You and agree for Your Divine blessing over them, their family and the community where they reside, in Jesus' name we pray, together.

Amen.

Loved Ones' Birth Days or Other Requests

____

____

____

____

March 18

Our wonderful Father in Heaven, we bring to You ALL of Your children who were born on March the 18th and we ask for Your blessings in their lives. We ask that they would know Your love and care as well as Your great plans for them. We ask for You to provide for them and their families, for You to put love and forgiveness in their hearts and for You to keep them safe. We give each one of them to You and agree for Your Divine blessing over them, their family and the community where they reside, in Jesus' name we pray, together.
Amen.

Loved Ones' Birth Days or Other Requests

____

____

____

____

March 19

Our wonderful Father in Heaven, we bring to You ALL of Your children who were born on March the 19th and we ask for Your blessings in their lives. We ask that they would know Your love and care as well as Your great plans for them. We ask for You to provide for them and their families, for You to put love and forgiveness in their hearts and for You to keep them safe. We give each one of them to You and agree for Your Divine blessing over them, their family and the community where they reside, in Jesus' name we pray, together.
Amen.

Loved Ones' Birth Days or Other Requests

____

____

____

____

March 20

Our wonderful Father in Heaven, we bring to You ALL of Your children who were born on March the 20th and we ask for Your blessings in their lives. We ask that they would know Your love and care as well as Your great plans for them. We ask for You to provide for them and their families, for You to put love and forgiveness in their hearts and for You to keep them safe. We give each one of them to You and agree for Your Divine blessing over them, their family and the community where they reside, in Jesus' name we pray, together.

Amen.

Loved Ones' Birth Days or Other Requests

____

____

____

____

March 21

Our wonderful Father in Heaven, we bring to You ALL of Your children who were born on March the 21st and we ask for Your blessings in their lives. We ask that they would know Your love and care as well as Your great plans for them. We ask for You to provide for them and their families, for You to put love and forgiveness in their hearts and for You to keep them safe. We give each one of them to You and agree for Your Divine blessing over them, their family and the community where they reside, in Jesus' name we pray, together.
Amen.

Loved Ones' Birth Days or Other Requests

____

____

____

____

March 22

Our wonderful Father in Heaven, we bring to You ALL of Your children who were born on March the 22nd and we ask for Your blessings in their lives. We ask that they would know Your love and care as well as Your great plans for them. We ask for You to provide for them and their families, for You to put love and forgiveness in their hearts and for You to keep them safe. We give each one of them to You and agree for Your Divine blessing over them, their family and the community where they reside, in Jesus' name we pray, together.
Amen.

Loved Ones' Birth Days or Other Requests

____

____

____

____

March 23

Our wonderful Father in Heaven, we bring to You ALL of Your children who were born on March 23rd and we ask for Your blessings in their lives. We ask that they would know Your love and care as well as Your great plans for them. We ask for You to provide for them and their families, for You to put love and forgiveness in their hearts and for You to keep them safe. We give each one of them to You and agree for Your Divine blessing over them, their family and the community where they reside, in Jesus' name we pray, together.
Amen.

Loved Ones' Birth Days or Other Requests

____

____

____

____

March 24

Our wonderful Father in Heaven, we bring to You ALL of Your children who were born on March the 24th and we ask for Your blessings in their lives. We ask that they would know Your love and care as well as Your great plans for them. We ask for You to provide for them and their families, for You to put love and forgiveness in their hearts and for You to keep them safe. We give each one of them to You and agree for Your Divine blessing over them, their family and the community where they reside, in Jesus' name we pray, together.

Amen.

Loved Ones' Birth Days or Other Requests

____

____

____

____

March 25

Our wonderful Father in Heaven, we bring to You ALL of Your children who were born on March the 25th and we ask for Your blessings in their lives. We ask that they would know Your love and care as well as Your great plans for them. We ask for You to provide for them and their families, for You to put love and forgiveness in their hearts and for You to keep them safe. We give each one of them to You and agree for Your Divine blessing over them, their family and the community where they reside, in Jesus' name we pray, together.
Amen.

Loved Ones' Birth Days or Other Requests

____

____

____

____

March 26

Our wonderful Father in Heaven, we bring to You ALL of Your children who were born on March the 26th and we ask for Your blessings in their lives. We ask that they would know Your love and care as well as Your great plans for them. We ask for You to provide for them and their families, for You to put love and forgiveness in their hearts and for You to keep them safe. We give each one of them to You and agree for Your Divine blessing over them, their family and the community where they reside, in Jesus' name we pray, together.

Amen.

Loved Ones' Birth Days or Other Requests

____

____

____

____

March 27

Our wonderful Father in Heaven, we bring to You ALL of Your children who were born on March the 27th and we ask for Your blessings in their lives. We ask that they would know Your love and care as well as Your great plans for them. We ask for You to provide for them and their families, for You to put love and forgiveness in their hearts and for You to keep them safe. We give each one of them to You and agree for Your Divine blessing over them, their family and the community where they reside, in Jesus' name we pray, together.
Amen.

Loved Ones' Birth Days or Other Requests

____

____

____

____

March 28

Our wonderful Father in Heaven, we bring to You ALL of Your children who were born on March the 28th and we ask for Your blessings in their lives. We ask that they would know Your love and care as well as Your great plans for them. We ask for You to provide for them and their families, for You to put love and forgiveness in their hearts and for You to keep them safe. We give each one of them to You and agree for Your Divine blessing over them, their family and the community where they reside, in Jesus' name we pray, together.

Amen.

Loved Ones' Birth Days or Other Requests

____

____

____

____

March 29

Our wonderful Father in Heaven, we bring to You ALL of Your children who were born on March the 29th and we ask for Your blessings in their lives. We ask that they would know Your love and care as well as Your great plans for them. We ask for You to provide for them and their families, for You to put love and forgiveness in their hearts and for You to keep them safe. We give each one of them to You and agree for Your Divine blessing over them, their family and the community where they reside, in Jesus' name we pray, together.

Amen.

Loved Ones' Birth Days or Other Requests

____

____

____

____

March 30

Our wonderful Father in Heaven, we bring to You ALL of Your children who were born on March the 30th and we ask for Your blessings in their lives. We ask that they would know Your love and care as well as Your great plans for them. We ask for You to provide for them and their families, for You to put love and forgiveness in their hearts and for You to keep them safe. We give each one of them to You and agree for Your Divine blessing over them, their family and the community where they reside, in Jesus' name we pray, together.
Amen.

Loved Ones' Birth Days or Other Requests

____

____

____

____

March 31

Our wonderful Father in Heaven, we bring to You ALL of Your children who were born on March the 31st and we ask for Your blessings in their lives. We ask that they would know Your love and care as well as Your great plans for them. We ask for You to provide for them and their families, for You to put love and forgiveness in their hearts and for You to keep them safe. We give each one of them to You and agree for Your Divine blessing over them, their family and the community where they reside, in Jesus' name we pray, together.
Amen.

Loved Ones' Birth Days or Other Requests

____

____

____

____

April 1

Our wonderful Father in Heaven, we bring to You ALL of Your children who were born on April the 1st and we ask for Your blessings in their lives. We ask that they would know Your love and care as well as Your great plans for them. We ask for You to provide for them and their families, for You to put love and forgiveness in their hearts and for You to keep them safe. We give each one of them to You and agree for Your Divine blessing over them, their family and the community where they reside, in Jesus' name we pray, together.
Amen.

Loved Ones' Birth Days or Other Requests

____

____

____

____

April 2

Our wonderful Father in Heaven, we bring to You ALL of Your children who were born on April the 2nd and we ask for Your blessings in their lives. We ask that they would know Your love and care as well as Your great plans for them. We ask for You to provide for them and their families, for You to put love and forgiveness in their hearts and for You to keep them safe. We give each one of them to You and agree for Your Divine blessing over them, their family and the community where they reside, in Jesus' name we pray, together.
Amen.

Loved Ones' Birth Days or Other Requests

____

____

____

____

April 3

Our wonderful Father in Heaven, we bring to You ALL of Your children who were born on April the 3rd and we ask for Your blessings in their lives. We ask that they would know Your love and care as well as Your great plans for them. We ask for You to provide for them and their families, for You to put love and forgiveness in their hearts and for You to keep them safe. We give each one of them to You and agree for Your Divine blessing over them, their family and the community where they reside, in Jesus' name we pray, together.
Amen.

Loved Ones' Birth Days or Other Requests

____

____

____

____

April 4

Our wonderful Father in Heaven, we bring to You ALL of Your children who were born on April the 4th and we ask for Your blessings in their lives. We ask that they would know Your love and care as well as Your great plans for them. We ask for You to provide for them and their families, for You to put love and forgiveness in their hearts and for You to keep them safe. We give each one of them to You and agree for Your Divine blessing over them, their family and the community where they reside, in Jesus' name we pray, together.

Amen.

Loved Ones' Birth Days or Other Requests

____

____

____

____

April 5

Our wonderful Father in Heaven, we bring to You ALL of Your children who were born on April the 5th and we ask for Your blessings in their lives. We ask that they would know Your love and care as well as Your great plans for them. We ask for You to provide for them and their families, for You to put love and forgiveness in their hearts and for You to keep them safe. We give each one of them to You and agree for Your Divine blessing over them, their family and the community where they reside, in Jesus' name we pray, together.

Amen.

Loved Ones' Birth Days or Other Requests

____

____

____

____

April 6

Our wonderful Father in Heaven, we bring to You ALL of Your children who were born on April the 6th and we ask for Your blessings in their lives. We ask that they would know Your love and care as well as Your great plans for them. We ask for You to provide for them and their families, for You to put love and forgiveness in their hearts and for You to keep them safe. We give each one of them to You and agree for Your Divine blessing over them, their family and the community where they reside, in Jesus' name we pray, together.
Amen.

Loved Ones' Birth Days or Other Requests

____

____

____

____

April 7

Our wonderful Father in Heaven, we bring to You ALL of Your children who were born on April the 7th and we ask for Your blessings in their lives. We ask that they would know Your love and care as well as Your great plans for them. We ask for You to provide for them and their families, for You to put love and forgiveness in their hearts and for You to keep them safe. We give each one of them to You and agree for Your Divine blessing over them, their family and the community where they reside, in Jesus' name we pray, together.

Amen.

Loved Ones' Birth Days or Other Requests

____

____

____

____

April 8

Our wonderful Father in Heaven, we bring to You ALL of Your children who were born on April the 8th and we ask for Your blessings in their lives. We ask that they would know Your love and care as well as Your great plans for them. We ask for You to provide for them and their families, for You to put love and forgiveness in their hearts and for You to keep them safe. We give each one of them to You and agree for Your Divine blessing over them, their family and the community where they reside, in Jesus' name we pray, together.

Amen.

Loved Ones' Birth Days or Other Requests

____

____

____

____

April 9

Our wonderful Father in Heaven, we bring to You ALL of Your children who were born on April the 9th and we ask for Your blessings in their lives. We ask that they would know Your love and care as well as Your great plans for them. We ask for You to provide for them and their families, for You to put love and forgiveness in their hearts and for You to keep them safe. We give each one of them to You and agree for Your Divine blessing over them, their family and the community where they reside, in Jesus' name we pray, together.

Amen.

Loved Ones' Birth Days or Other Requests

____

____

____

____

April 10

Our wonderful Father in Heaven, we bring to You ALL of Your children who were born on April the 10th and we ask for Your blessings in their lives. We ask that they would know Your love and care as well as Your great plans for them. We ask for You to provide for them and their families, for You to put love and forgiveness in their hearts and for You to keep them safe. We give each one of them to You and agree for Your Divine blessing over them, their family and the community where they reside, in Jesus' name we pray, together.

Amen.

Loved Ones' Birth Days or Other Requests

____

____

____

____

April 11

Our wonderful Father in Heaven, we bring to You ALL of Your children who were born on April the 11th and we ask for Your blessings in their lives. We ask that they would know Your love and care as well as Your great plans for them. We ask for You to provide for them and their families, for You to put love and forgiveness in their hearts and for You to keep them safe. We give each one of them to You and agree for Your Divine blessing over them, their family and the community where they reside, in Jesus' name we pray, together.

Amen.

Loved Ones' Birth Days or Other Requests

____

____

____

____

April 12

Our wonderful Father in Heaven, we bring to You ALL of Your children who were born on April the 12th and we ask for Your blessings in their lives. We ask that they would know Your love and care as well as Your great plans for them. We ask for You to provide for them and their families, for You to put love and forgiveness in their hearts and for You to keep them safe. We give each one of them to You and agree for Your Divine blessing over them, their family and the community where they reside, in Jesus' name we pray, together.

Amen.

Loved Ones' Birth Days or Other Requests

____

____

____

____

April 13

Our wonderful Father in Heaven, we bring to You ALL of Your children who were born on April the 13th and we ask for Your blessings in their lives. We ask that they would know Your love and care as well as Your great plans for them. We ask for You to provide for them and their families, for You to put love and forgiveness in their hearts and for You to keep them safe. We give each one of them to You and agree for Your Divine blessing over them, their family and the community where they reside, in Jesus' name we pray, together.
Amen.

Loved Ones' Birth Days or Other Requests

____

____

____

____

April 14

Our wonderful Father in Heaven, we bring to You ALL of Your children who were born on April the 14th and we ask for Your blessings in their lives. We ask that they would know Your love and care as well as Your great plans for them. We ask for You to provide for them and their families, for You to put love and forgiveness in their hearts and for You to keep them safe. We give each one of them to You and agree for Your Divine blessing over them, their family and the community where they reside, in Jesus' name we pray, together.

Amen.

Loved Ones' Birth Days or Other Requests

____

____

____

____

April 15

Our wonderful Father in Heaven, we bring to You ALL of Your children who were born on April the 15th and we ask for Your blessings in their lives. We ask that they would know Your love and care as well as Your great plans for them. We ask for You to provide for them and their families, for You to put love and forgiveness in their hearts and for You to keep them safe. We give each one of them to You and agree for Your Divine blessing over them, their family and the community where they reside, in Jesus' name we pray, together.

Amen.

Loved Ones' Birth Days or Other Requests

____

____

____

____

April 16

Our wonderful Father in Heaven, we bring to You ALL of Your children who were born on April the 16th and we ask for Your blessings in their lives. We ask that they would know Your love and care as well as Your great plans for them. We ask for You to provide for them and their families, for You to put love and forgiveness in their hearts and for You to keep them safe. We give each one of them to You and agree for Your Divine blessing over them, their family and the community where they reside, in Jesus' name we pray, together.

Amen.

Loved Ones' Birth Days or Other Requests

____

____

____

____

April 17

Our wonderful Father in Heaven, we bring to You ALL of Your children who were born on April the 17th and we ask for Your blessings in their lives. We ask that they would know Your love and care as well as Your great plans for them. We ask for You to provide for them and their families, for You to put love and forgiveness in their hearts and for You to keep them safe. We give each one of them to You and agree for Your Divine blessing over them, their famlly and the community where they reside, in Jesus' name we pray, together.

Amen.

Loved Ones' Birth Days or Other Requests

____

____

____

____

April 18

Our wonderful Father in Heaven, we bring to You ALL of Your children who were born on April the 18th and we ask for Your blessings in their lives. We ask that they would know Your love and care as well as Your great plans for them. We ask for You to provide for them and their families, for You to put love and forgiveness in their hearts and for You to keep them safe. We give each one of them to You and agree for Your Divine blessing over them, their family and the community where they reside, in Jesus' name we pray, together.
Amen.

Loved Ones' Birth Days or Other Requests

____

____

____

____

April 19

Our wonderful Father in Heaven, we bring to You ALL of Your children who were born on April the 19th and we ask for Your blessings in their lives. We ask that they would know Your love and care as well as Your great plans for them. We ask for You to provide for them and their families, for You to put love and forgiveness in their hearts and for You to keep them safe. We give each one of them to You and agree for Your Divine blessing over them, their family and the community where they reside, in Jesus' name we pray, together.

Amen.

Loved Ones' Birth Days or Other Requests

____

____

____

____

April 20

Our wonderful Father in Heaven, we bring to You ALL of Your children who were born on April the 20th and we ask for Your blessings in their lives. We ask that they would know Your love and care as well as Your great plans for them. We ask for You to provide for them and their families, for You to put love and forgiveness in their hearts and for You to keep them safe. We give each one of them to You and agree for Your Divine blessing over them, their family and the community where they reside, in Jesus' name we pray, together.

Amen.

Loved Ones' Birth Days or Other Requests

____

____

____

____

April 21

Our wonderful Father in Heaven, we bring to You ALL of Your children who were born on April the 21st and we ask for Your blessings in their lives. We ask that they would know Your love and care as well as Your great plans for them. We ask for You to provide for them and their families, for You to put love and forgiveness in their hearts and for You to keep them safe. We give each one of them to You and agree for Your Divine blessing over them, their family and the community where they reside, in Jesus' name we pray, together.

Amen.

Loved Ones' Birth Days or Other Requests

____

____

____

____

April 22

Our wonderful Father in Heaven, we bring to You ALL of Your children who were born on April the 22nd and we ask for Your blessings in their lives. We ask that they would know Your love and care as well as Your great plans for them. We ask for You to provide for them and their families, for You to put love and forgiveness in their hearts and for You to keep them safe. We give each one of them to You and agree for Your Divine blessing over them, their family and the community where they reside, in Jesus' name we pray, together.

Amen.

Loved Ones' Birth Days or Other Requests

____

____

____

____

April 23

Our wonderful Father in Heaven, we bring to You ALL of Your children who were born on April the 23rd and we ask for Your blessings in their lives. We ask that they would know Your love and care as well as Your great plans for them. We ask for You to provide for them and their families, for You to put love and forgiveness in their hearts and for You to keep them safe. We give each one of them to You and agree for Your Divine blessing over them, their famlly and the community where they reside, in Jesus' name we pray, together.

Amen.

Loved Ones' Birth Days or Other Requests

____

____

____

____

April 24

Our wonderful Father in Heaven, we bring to You ALL of Your children who were born on April the 24th and we ask for Your blessings in their lives. We ask that they would know Your love and care as well as Your great plans for them. We ask for You to provide for them and their families, for You to put love and forgiveness in their hearts and for You to keep them safe. We give each one of them to You and agree for Your Divine blessing over them, their family and the community where they reside, in Jesus' name we pray, together.

Amen.

Loved Ones' Birth Days or Other Requests

____

____

____

____

April 25

Our wonderful Father in Heaven, we bring to You ALL of Your children who were born on April the 25th and we ask for Your blessings in their lives. We ask that they would know Your love and care as well as Your great plans for them. We ask for You to provide for them and their families, for You to put love and forgiveness in their hearts and for You to keep them safe. We give each one of them to You and agree for Your Divine blessing over them, their family and the community where they reside, in Jesus' name we pray, together.

Amen.

Loved Ones' Birth Days or Other Requests

____

____

____

____

April 26

Our wonderful Father in Heaven, we bring to You ALL of Your children who were born on April the 26th and we ask for Your blessings in their lives. We ask that they would know Your love and care as well as Your great plans for them. We ask for You to provide for them and their families, for You to put love and forgiveness in their hearts and for You to keep them safe. We give each one of them to You and agree for Your Divine blessing over them, their family and the community where they reside, in Jesus' name we pray, together.
Amen.

Loved Ones' Birth Days or Other Requests

____

____

____

____

April 27

Our wonderful Father in Heaven, we bring to You ALL of Your children who were born on April the 27th and we ask for Your blessings in their lives. We ask that they would know Your love and care as well as Your great plans for them. We ask for You to provide for them and their families, for You to put love and forgiveness in their hearts and for You to keep them safe. We give each one of them to You and agree for Your Divine blessing over them, their family and the community where they reside, in Jesus' name we pray, together.

Amen.

Loved Ones' Birth Days or Other Requests

____

____

____

____

April 28

Our wonderful Father in Heaven, we bring to You ALL of Your children who were born on April the 28th and we ask for Your blessings in their lives. We ask that they would know Your love and care as well as Your great plans for them. We ask for You to provide for them and their families, for You to put love and forgiveness in their hearts and for You to keep them safe. We give each one of them to You and agree for Your Divine blessing over them, their family and the community where they reside, in Jesus' name we pray, together.

Amen.

Loved Ones' Birth Days or Other Requests

____

____

____

____

April 29

Our wonderful Father in Heaven, we bring to You ALL of Your children who were born on April the 29th and we ask for Your blessings in their lives. We ask that they would know Your love and care as well as Your great plans for them. We ask for You to provide for them and their families, for You to put love and forgiveness in their hearts and for You to keep them safe. We give each one of them to You and agree for Your Divine blessing over them, their family and the community where they reside, in Jesus' name we pray, together.
Amen.

Loved Ones' Birth Days or Other Requests

____

____

____

____

April 30

Our wonderful Father in Heaven, we bring to You ALL of Your children who were born on April the 30th and we ask for Your blessings in their lives. We ask that they would know Your love and care as well as Your great plans for them. We ask for You to provide for them and their families, for You to put love and forgiveness in their hearts and for You to keep them safe. We give each one of them to You and agree for Your Divine blessing over them, their family and the community where they reside, in Jesus' name we pray, together.
Amen.

Loved Ones' Birth Days or Other Requests

____

____

____

____

May 1

Our wonderful Father in Heaven, we bring to You ALL of Your children who were born on May the 1st and we ask for Your blessings in their lives. We ask that they would know Your love and care as well as Your great plans for them. We ask for You to provide for them and their families, for You to put love and forgiveness in their hearts and for You to keep them safe. We give each one of them to You and agree for Your Divine blessing over them, their family and the community where they reside, in Jesus' name we pray, together.

Amen.

Loved Ones' Birth Days or Other Requests

____

____

____

____

May 2

Our wonderful Father in Heaven, we bring to You ALL of Your children who were born on May the 2nd and we ask for Your blessings in their lives. We ask that they would know Your love and care as well as Your great plans for them. We ask for You to provide for them and their families, for You to put love and forgiveness in their hearts and for You to keep them safe. We give each one of them to You and agree for Your Divine blessing over them, their family and the community where they reside, in Jesus' name we pray, together.
Amen.

Loved Ones' Birth Days or Other Requests

____

____

____

____

May 3

Our wonderful Father in Heaven, we bring to You ALL of Your children who were born on May the 3rd and we ask for Your blessings in their lives. We ask that they would know Your love and care as well as Your great plans for them. We ask for You to provide for them and their families, for You to put love and forgiveness in their hearts and for You to keep them safe. We give each one of them to You and agree for Your Divine blessing over them, their family and the community where they reside, in Jesus' name we pray, together.

Amen.

Loved Ones' Birth Days or Other Requests

____

____

____

____

May 4

Our wonderful Father in Heaven, we bring to You ALL of Your children who were born on May the 4th and we ask for Your blessings in their lives. We ask that they would know Your love and care as well as Your great plans for them. We ask for You to provide for them and their families, for You to put love and forgiveness in their hearts and for You to keep them safe. We give each one of them to You and agree for Your Divine blessing over them, their family and the community where they reside, in Jesus' name we pray, together.

Amen.

Loved Ones' Birth Days or Other Requests

____

____

____

____

May 5

Our wonderful Father in Heaven, we bring to You ALL of Your children who were born on May the 5th and we ask for Your blessings in their lives. We ask that they would know Your love and care as well as Your great plans for them. We ask for You to provide for them and their families, for You to put love and forgiveness in their hearts and for You to keep them safe. We give each one of them to You and agree for Your Divine blessing over them, their family and the community where they reside, in Jesus' name we pray, together.

Amen.

Loved Ones' Birth Days or Other Requests

____

____

____

____

May 6

Our wonderful Father in Heaven, we bring to You ALL of Your children who were born on May the 6th and we ask for Your blessings in their lives. We ask that they would know Your love and care as well as Your great plans for them. We ask for You to provide for them and their families, for You to put love and forgiveness in their hearts and for You to keep them safe. We give each one of them to You and agree for Your Divine blessing over them, their family and the community where they reside, in Jesus' name we pray, together.
Amen.

Loved Ones' Birth Days or Other Requests

____

____

____

____

May 7

Our wonderful Father in Heaven, we bring to You ALL of Your children who were born on May the 7th and we ask for Your blessings in their lives. We ask that they would know Your love and care as well as Your great plans for them. We ask for You to provide for them and their families, for You to put love and forgiveness in their hearts and for You to keep them safe. We give each one of them to You and agree for Your Divine blessing over them, their family and the community where they reside, in Jesus' name we pray, together.

Amen.

Loved Ones' Birth Days or Other Requests

____

____

____

____

May 8

Our wonderful Father in Heaven, we bring to You ALL of Your children who were born on May the 8th and we ask for Your blessings in their lives. We ask that they would know Your love and care as well as Your great plans for them. We ask for You to provide for them and their families, for You to put love and forgiveness in their hearts and for You to keep them safe. We give each one of them to You and agree for Your Divine blessing over them, their family and the community where they reside, in Jesus' name we pray, together.
Amen.

Loved Ones' Birth Days or Other Requests

____

____

____

____

May 9

Our wonderful Father in Heaven, we bring to You ALL of Your children who were born on May the 9th and we ask for Your blessings in their lives. We ask that they would know Your love and care as well as Your great plans for them. We ask for You to provide for them and their families, for You to put love and forgiveness in their hearts and for You to keep them safe. We give each one of them to You and agree for Your Divine blessing over them, their family and the community where they reside, in Jesus' name we pray, together.
Amen.

Loved Ones' Birth Days or Other Requests

____

____

____

____

May 10

Our wonderful Father in Heaven, we bring to You ALL of Your children who were born on May the 10th and we ask for Your blessings in their lives. We ask that they would know Your love and care as well as Your great plans for them. We ask for You to provide for them and their families, for You to put love and forgiveness in their hearts and for You to keep them safe. We give each one of them to You and agree for Your Divine blessing over them, their family and the community where they reside, in Jesus' name we pray, together.

Amen.

Loved Ones' Birth Days or Other Requests

____

____

____

____

May 11

Our wonderful Father in Heaven, we bring to You ALL of Your children who were born on May the 11th and we ask for Your blessings in their lives. We ask that they would know Your love and care as well as Your great plans for them. We ask for You to provide for them and their families, for You to put love and forgiveness in their hearts and for You to keep them safe. We give each one of them to You and agree for Your Divine blessing over them, their family and the community where they reside, in Jesus' name we pray, together.

Amen.

Loved Ones' Birth Days or Other Requests

____

____

____

____

May 12

Our wonderful Father in Heaven, we bring to You ALL of Your children who were born on May the 12th and we ask for Your blessings in their lives. We ask that they would know Your love and care as well as Your great plans for them. We ask for You to provide for them and their families, for You to put love and forgiveness in their hearts and for You to keep them safe. We give each one of them to You and agree for Your Divine blessing over them, their family and the community where they reside, in Jesus' name we pray, together.
Amen.

Loved Ones' Birth Days or Other Requests

____

____

____

____

May 13

Our wonderful Father in Heaven, we bring to You ALL of Your children who were born on May the 13th and we ask for Your blessings in their lives. We ask that they would know Your love and care as well as Your great plans for them. We ask for You to provide for them and their families, for You to put love and forgiveness in their hearts and for You to keep them safe. We give each one of them to You and agree for Your Divine blessing over them, their family and the community where they reside, in Jesus' name we pray, together.

Amen.

Loved Ones' Birth Days or Other Requests

____

____

____

____

May 14

Our wonderful Father in Heaven, we bring to You ALL of Your children who were born on May the 14th and we ask for Your blessings in their lives. We ask that they would know Your love and care as well as Your great plans for them. We ask for You to provide for them and their families, for You to put love and forgiveness in their hearts and for You to keep them safe. We give each one of them to You and agree for Your Divine blessing over them, their family and the community where they reside, in Jesus' name we pray, together.
Amen.

Loved Ones' Birth Days or Other Requests

____

____

____

____

May 15

Our wonderful Father in Heaven, we bring to You ALL of Your children who were born on May the 15th and we ask for Your blessings in their lives. We ask that they would know Your love and care as well as Your great plans for them. We ask for You to provide for them and their families, for You to put love and forgiveness in their hearts and for You to keep them safe. We give each one of them to You and agree for Your Divine blessing over them, their family and the community where they reside, in Jesus' name we pray, together.
Amen.

Loved Ones' Birth Days or Other Requests

____

____

____

____

May 16

Our wonderful Father in Heaven, we bring to You ALL of Your children who were born on May the 16th and we ask for Your blessings in their lives. We ask that they would know Your love and care as well as Your great plans for them. We ask for You to provide for them and their families, for You to put love and forgiveness in their hearts and for You to keep them safe. We give each one of them to You and agree for Your Divine blessing over them, their family and the community where they reside, in Jesus' name we pray, together.
Amen.

Loved Ones' Birth Days or Other Requests

____

____

____

____

May 17

Our wonderful Father in Heaven, we bring to You ALL of Your children who were born on May the 17th and we ask for Your blessings in their lives. We ask that they would know Your love and care as well as Your great plans for them. We ask for You to provide for them and their families, for You to put love and forgiveness in their hearts and for You to keep them safe. We give each one of them to You and agree for Your Divine blessing over them, their family and the community where they reside, in Jesus' name we pray, together.

Amen.

Loved Ones' Birth Days or Other Requests

____

____

____

____

May 18

Our wonderful Father in Heaven, we bring to You ALL of Your children who were born on May the 18th and we ask for Your blessings in their lives. We ask that they would know Your love and care as well as Your great plans for them. We ask for You to provide for them and their families, for You to put love and forgiveness in their hearts and for You to keep them safe. We give each one of them to You and agree for Your Divine blessing over them, their family and the community where they reside, in Jesus' name we pray, together.

Amen.

Loved Ones' Birth Days or Other Requests

____

____

____

____

May 19

Our wonderful Father in Heaven, we bring to You ALL of Your children who were born on May the 19th and we ask for Your blessings in their lives. We ask that they would know Your love and care as well as Your great plans for them. We ask for You to provide for them and their families, for You to put love and forgiveness in their hearts and for You to keep them safe. We give each one of them to You and agree for Your Divine blessing over them, their family and the community where they reside, in Jesus' name we pray, together.

Amen.

Loved Ones' Birth Days or Other Requests

____

____

____

____

May 20

Our wonderful Father in Heaven, we bring to You ALL of Your children who were born on May the 20th and we ask for Your blessings in their lives. We ask that they would know Your love and care as well as Your great plans for them. We ask for You to provide for them and their families, for You to put love and forgiveness in their hearts and for You to keep them safe. We give each one of them to You and agree for Your Divine blessing over them, their family and the community where they reside, in Jesus' name we pray, together.

Amen.

Loved Ones' Birth Days or Other Requests

____

____

____

____

May 21

Our wonderful Father in Heaven, we bring to You ALL of Your children who were born on May the 21st and we ask for Your blessings in their lives. We ask that they would know Your love and care as well as Your great plans for them. We ask for You to provide for them and their families, for You to put love and forgiveness in their hearts and for You to keep them safe. We give each one of them to You and agree for Your Divine blessing over them, their family and the community where they reside, in Jesus' name we pray, together.

Amen.

Loved Ones' Birth Days or Other Requests

____

____

____

____

May 22

Our wonderful Father in Heaven, we bring to You ALL of Your children who were born on May the 22nd and we ask for Your blessings in their lives. We ask that they would know Your love and care as well as Your great plans for them. We ask for You to provide for them and their families, for You to put love and forgiveness in their hearts and for You to keep them safe. We give each one of them to You and agree for Your Divine blessing over them, their family and the community where they reside, in Jesus' name we pray, together.
Amen.

Loved Ones' Birth Days or Other Requests

____

____

____

____

May 23

Our wonderful Father in Heaven, we bring to You ALL of Your children who were born on May the 23rd and we ask for Your blessings in their lives. We ask that they would know Your love and care as well as Your great plans for them. We ask for You to provide for them and their families, for You to put love and forgiveness in their hearts and for You to keep them safe. We give each one of them to You and agree for Your Divine blessing over them, their family and the community where they reside, in Jesus' name we pray, together.

Amen.

Loved Ones' Birth Days or Other Requests

____

____

____

____

May 24

Our wonderful Father in Heaven, we bring to You ALL of Your children who were born on May the 24th and we ask for Your blessings in their lives. We ask that they would know Your love and care as well as Your great plans for them. We ask for You to provide for them and their families, for You to put love and forgiveness in their hearts and for You to keep them safe. We give each one of them to You and agree for Your Divine blessing over them, their family and the community where they reside, in Jesus' name we pray, together.
Amen.

Loved Ones' Birth Days or Other Requests

____

____

____

____

May 25

Our wonderful Father in Heaven, we bring to You ALL of Your children who were born on May the 25th and we ask for Your blessings in their lives. We ask that they would know Your love and care as well as Your great plans for them. We ask for You to provide for them and their families, for You to put love and forgiveness in their hearts and for You to keep them safe. We give each one of them to You and agree for Your Divine blessing over them, their family and the community where they reside, in Jesus' name we pray, together.
Amen.

Loved Ones' Birth Days or Other Requests

____

____

____

____

May 26

Our wonderful Father in Heaven, we bring to You ALL of Your children who were born on May the 26th and we ask for Your blessings in their lives. We ask that they would know Your love and care as well as Your great plans for them. We ask for You to provide for them and their families, for You to put love and forgiveness in their hearts and for You to keep them safe. We give each one of them to You and agree for Your Divine blessing over them, their family and the community where they reside, in Jesus' name we pray, together.
Amen.

Loved Ones' Birth Days or Other Requests

____

____

____

____

May 27

Our wonderful Father in Heaven, we bring to You ALL of Your children who were born on May the 27th and we ask for Your blessings in their lives. We ask that they would know Your love and care as well as Your great plans for them. We ask for You to provide for them and their families, for You to put love and forgiveness in their hearts and for You to keep them safe. We give each one of them to You and agree for Your Divine blessing over them, their family and the community where they reside, in Jesus' name we pray, together.
Amen.

Loved Ones' Birth Days or Other Requests

____

____

____

____

May 28

Our wonderful Father in Heaven, we bring to You ALL of Your children who were born on May the 28th and we ask for Your blessings in their lives. We ask that they would know Your love and care as well as Your great plans for them. We ask for You to provide for them and their families, for You to put love and forgiveness in their hearts and for You to keep them safe. We give each one of them to You and agree for Your Divine blessing over them, their family and the community where they reside, in Jesus' name we pray, together.
Amen.

Loved Ones' Birth Days or Other Requests

____

____

____

____

May 29

Our wonderful Father in Heaven, we bring to You ALL of Your children who were born on May the 29th and we ask for Your blessings in their lives. We ask that they would know Your love and care as well as Your great plans for them. We ask for You to provide for them and their families, for You to put love and forgiveness in their hearts and for You to keep them safe. We give each one of them to You and agree for Your Divine blessing over them, their family and the community where they reside, in Jesus' name we pray, together.

Amen.

Loved Ones' Birth Days or Other Requests

____

____

____

____

May 30

Our wonderful Father in Heaven, we bring to You ALL of Your children who were born on May the 30th and we ask for Your blessings in their lives. We ask that they would know Your love and care as well as Your great plans for them. We ask for You to provide for them and their families, for You to put love and forgiveness in their hearts and for You to keep them safe. We give each one of them to You and agree for Your Divine blessing over them, their family and the community where they reside, in Jesus' name we pray, together.
Amen.

Loved Ones' Birth Days or Other Requests

____

____

____

____

May 31

Our wonderful Father in Heaven, we bring to You ALL of Your children who were born on May the 31st and we ask for Your blessings in their lives. We ask that they would know Your love and care as well as Your great plans for them. We ask for You to provide for them and their families, for You to put love and forgiveness in their hearts and for You to keep them safe. We give each one of them to You and agree for Your Divine blessing over them, their family and the community where they reside, in Jesus' name we pray, together.

Amen.

Loved Ones' Birth Days or Other Requests

____

____

____

____

June 1

Our wonderful Father in Heaven, we bring to You ALL of Your children who were born on June the 1st and we ask for Your blessings in their lives. We ask that they would know Your love and care as well as Your great plans for them. We ask for You to provide for them and their families, for You to put love and forgiveness in their hearts and for You to keep them safe. We give each one of them to You and agree for Your Divine blessing over them, their family and the community where they reside, in Jesus' name we pray, together.
Amen.

Loved Ones' Birth Days or Other Requests

____

____

____

____

June 2

Our wonderful Father in Heaven, we bring to You ALL of Your children who were born on June the 2nd and we ask for Your blessings in their lives. We ask that they would know Your love and care as well as Your great plans for them. We ask for You to provide for them and their families, for You to put love and forgiveness in their hearts and for You to keep them safe. We give each one of them to You and agree for Your Divine blessing over them, their family and the community where they reside, in Jesus' name we pray, together.

Amen.

Loved Ones' Birth Days or Other Requests

____

____

____

____

June 3

Our wonderful Father in Heaven, we bring to You ALL of Your children who were born on June the 3rd and we ask for Your blessings in their lives. We ask that they would know Your love and care as well as Your great plans for them. We ask for You to provide for them and their families, for You to put love and forgiveness in their hearts and for You to keep them safe. We give each one of them to You and agree for Your Divine blessing over them, their family and the community where they reside, in Jesus' name we pray, together.

Amen.

Loved Ones' Birth Days or Other Requests

____

____

____

____

June 4

Our wonderful Father in Heaven, we bring to You ALL of Your children who were born on June the 4th and we ask for Your blessings in their lives. We ask that they would know Your love and care as well as Your great plans for them. We ask for You to provide for them and their families, for You to put love and forgiveness in their hearts and for You to keep them safe. We give each one of them to You and agree for Your Divine blessing over them, their family and the community where they reside, in Jesus' name we pray, together.

Amen.

Loved Ones' Birth Days or Other Requests

____

____

____

____

June 5

Our wonderful Father in Heaven, we bring to You ALL of Your children who were born on June the 5th and we ask for Your blessings in their lives. We ask that they would know Your love and care as well as Your great plans for them. We ask for You to provide for them and their families, for You to put love and forgiveness in their hearts and for You to keep them safe. We give each one of them to You and agree for Your Divine blessing over them, their family and the community where they reside, in Jesus' name we pray, together.

Amen.

Loved Ones' Birth Days or Other Requests

____

____

____

____

June 6

Our wonderful Father in Heaven, we bring to You ALL of Your children who were born on June the 6th and we ask for Your blessings in their lives. We ask that they would know Your love and care as well as Your great plans for them. We ask for You to provide for them and their families, for You to put love and forgiveness in their hearts and for You to keep them safe. We give each one of them to You and agree for Your Divine blessing over them, their family and the community where they reside, in Jesus' name we pray, together.

Amen.

Loved Ones' Birth Days or Other Requests

____

____

____

____

June 7

Our wonderful Father in Heaven, we bring to You ALL of Your children who were born on June the 7th and we ask for Your blessings in their lives. We ask that they would know Your love and care as well as Your great plans for them. We ask for You to provide for them and their families, for You to put love and forgiveness in their hearts and for You to keep them safe. We give each one of them to You and agree for Your Divine blessing over them, their family and the community where they reside, in Jesus' name we pray, together.
Amen.

Loved Ones' Birth Days or Other Requests

____

____

____

____

June 8

Our wonderful Father in Heaven, we bring to You ALL of Your children who were born on June the 8th and we ask for Your blessings in their lives. We ask that they would know Your love and care as well as Your great plans for them. We ask for You to provide for them and their families, for You to put love and forgiveness in their hearts and for You to keep them safe. We give each one of them to You and agree for Your Divine blessing over them, their family and the community where they reside, in Jesus' name we pray, together.

Amen.

Loved Ones' Birth Days or Other Requests

____

____

____

____

June 9

Our wonderful Father in Heaven, we bring to You ALL of Your children who were born on June the 9th and we ask for Your blessings in their lives. We ask that they would know Your love and care as well as Your great plans for them. We ask for You to provide for them and their families, for You to put love and forgiveness in their hearts and for You to keep them safe. We give each one of them to You and agree for Your Divine blessing over them, their family and the community where they reside, in Jesus' name we pray, together.
Amen.

Loved Ones' Birth Days or Other Requests

____

____

____

____

June 10

Our wonderful Father in Heaven, we bring to You ALL of Your children who were born on June the 10th and we ask for Your blessings in their lives. We ask that they would know Your love and care as well as Your great plans for them. We ask for You to provide for them and their families, for You to put love and forgiveness in their hearts and for You to keep them safe. We give each one of them to You and agree for Your Divine blessing over them, their family and the community where they reside, in Jesus' name we pray, together.
Amen.

Loved Ones' Birth Days or Other Requests

____

____

____

____

June 11

Our wonderful Father in Heaven, we bring to You ALL of Your children who were born on June the 11th and we ask for Your blessings in their lives. We ask that they would know Your love and care as well as Your great plans for them. We ask for You to provide for them and their families, for You to put love and forgiveness in their hearts and for You to keep them safe. We give each one of them to You and agree for Your Divine blessing over them, their family and the community where they reside, in Jesus' name we pray, together.
Amen.

Loved Ones' Birth Days or Other Requests

____

____

____

____

June 12

Our wonderful Father in Heaven, we bring to You ALL of Your children who were born on June the 12th and we ask for Your blessings in their lives. We ask that they would know Your love and care as well as Your great plans for them. We ask for You to provide for them and their families, for You to put love and forgiveness in their hearts and for You to keep them safe. We give each one of them to You and agree for Your Divine blessing over them, their family and the community where they reside, in Jesus' name we pray, together.

Amen.

Loved Ones' Birth Days or Other Requests

____

____

____

____

June 13

Our wonderful Father in Heaven, we bring to You ALL of Your children who were born on June the 13th and we ask for Your blessings in their lives. We ask that they would know Your love and care as well as Your great plans for them. We ask for You to provide for them and their families, for You to put love and forgiveness in their hearts and for You to keep them safe. We give each one of them to You and agree for Your Divine blessing over them, their family and the community where they reside, in Jesus' name we pray, together.

Amen.

Loved Ones' Birth Days or Other Requests

____

____

____

____

June 14

Our wonderful Father in Heaven, we bring to You ALL of Your children who were born on June the 14th and we ask for Your blessings in their lives. We ask that they would know Your love and care as well as Your great plans for them. We ask for You to provide for them and their families, for You to put love and forgiveness in their hearts and for You to keep them safe. We give each one of them to You and agree for Your Divine blessing over them, their family and the community where they reside, in Jesus' name we pray, together.

Amen.

Loved Ones' Birth Days or Other Requests

____

____

____

____

June 15

Our wonderful Father in Heaven, we bring to You ALL of Your children who were born on June the 15th and we ask for Your blessings in their lives. We ask that they would know Your love and care as well as Your great plans for them. We ask for You to provide for them and their families, for You to put love and forgiveness in their hearts and for You to keep them safe. We give each one of them to You and agree for Your Divine blessing over them, their family and the community where they reside, in Jesus' name we pray, together.

Amen.

Loved Ones' Birth Days or Other Requests

____

____

____

____

June 16

Our wonderful Father in Heaven, we bring to You ALL of Your children who were born on June the 16th and we ask for Your blessings in their lives. We ask that they would know Your love and care as well as Your great plans for them. We ask for You to provide for them and their families, for You to put love and forgiveness in their hearts and for You to keep them safe. We give each one of them to You and agree for Your Divine blessing over them, their family and the community where they reside, in Jesus' name we pray, together.

Amen.

Loved Ones' Birth Days or Other Requests

____

____

____

____

June 17

Our wonderful Father in Heaven, we bring to You ALL of Your children who were born on June the 17th and we ask for Your blessings in their lives. We ask that they would know Your love and care as well as Your great plans for them. We ask for You to provide for them and their families, for You to put love and forgiveness in their hearts and for You to keep them safe. We give each one of them to You and agree for Your Divine blessing over them, their family and the community where they reside, in Jesus' name we pray, together.
Amen.

Loved Ones' Birth Days or Other Requests

____

____

____

____

June 18

Our wonderful Father in Heaven, we bring to You ALL of Your children who were born on June the 18th and we ask for Your blessings in their lives. We ask that they would know Your love and care as well as Your great plans for them. We ask for You to provide for them and their families, for You to put love and forgiveness in their hearts and for You to keep them safe. We give each one of them to You and agree for Your Divine blessing over them, their family and the community where they reside, in Jesus' name we pray, together.

Amen.

Loved Ones' Birth Days or Other Requests

____

____

____

____

June 19

Our wonderful Father in Heaven, we bring to You ALL of Your children who were born on June the 19th and we ask for Your blessings in their lives. We ask that they would know Your love and care as well as Your great plans for them. We ask for You to provide for them and their families, for You to put love and forgiveness in their hearts and for You to keep them safe. We give each one of them to You and agree for Your Divine blessing over them, their family and the community where they reside, in Jesus' name we pray, together.
Amen.

Loved Ones' Birth Days or Other Requests

____

____

____

____

June 20

Our wonderful Father in Heaven, we bring to You ALL of Your children who were born on June the 20th and we ask for Your blessings in their lives. We ask that they would know Your love and care as well as Your great plans for them. We ask for You to provide for them and their families, for You to put love and forgiveness in their hearts and for You to keep them safe. We give each one of them to You and agree for Your Divine blessing over them, their family and the community where they reside, in Jesus' name we pray, together.
Amen.

Loved Ones' Birth Days or Other Requests

____

____

____

____

June 21

Our wonderful Father in Heaven, we bring to You ALL of Your children who were born on June the 21st and we ask for Your blessings in their lives. We ask that they would know Your love and care as well as Your great plans for them. We ask for You to provide for them and their families, for You to put love and forgiveness in their hearts and for You to keep them safe. We give each one of them to You and agree for Your Divine blessing over them, their family and the community where they reside, in Jesus' name we pray, together.

Amen.

Loved Ones' Birth Days or Other Requests

____

____

____

____

June 22

Our wonderful Father in Heaven, we bring to You ALL of Your children who were born on June the 22nd and we ask for Your blessings in their lives. We ask that they would know Your love and care as well as Your great plans for them. We ask for You to provide for them and their families, for You to put love and forgiveness in their hearts and for You to keep them safe. We give each one of them to You and agree for Your Divine blessing over them, their family and the community where they reside, in Jesus' name we pray, together.

Amen.

Loved Ones' Birth Days or Other Requests

____

____

____

____

June 23

Our wonderful Father in Heaven, we bring to You ALL of Your children who were born on June the 23rd and we ask for Your blessings in their lives. We ask that they would know Your love and care as well as Your great plans for them. We ask for You to provide for them and their families, for You to put love and forgiveness in their hearts and for You to keep them safe. We give each one of them to You and agree for Your Divine blessing over them, their family and the community where they reside, in Jesus' name we pray, together.
Amen.

Loved Ones' Birth Days or Other Requests

____

____

____

____

June 24

Our wonderful Father in Heaven, we bring to You ALL of Your children who were born on June the 24th and we ask for Your blessings in their lives. We ask that they would know Your love and care as well as Your great plans for them. We ask for You to provide for them and their families, for You to put love and forgiveness in their hearts and for You to keep them safe. We give each one of them to You and agree for Your Divine blessing over them, their family and the community where they reside, in Jesus' name we pray, together.

Amen.

Loved Ones' Birth Days or Other Requests

____

____

____

____

June 25

Our wonderful Father in Heaven, we bring to You ALL of Your children who were born on June the 25th and we ask for Your blessings in their lives. We ask that they would know Your love and care as well as Your great plans for them. We ask for You to provide for them and their families, for You to put love and forgiveness in their hearts and for You to keep them safe. We give each one of them to You and agree for Your Divine blessing over them, their family and the community where they reside, in Jesus' name we pray, together.
Amen.

Loved Ones' Birth Days or Other Requests

____

____

____

____

June 26

Our wonderful Father in Heaven, we bring to You ALL of Your children who were born on June the 26th and we ask for Your blessings in their lives. We ask that they would know Your love and care as well as Your great plans for them. We ask for You to provide for them and their families, for You to put love and forgiveness in their hearts and for You to keep them safe. We give each one of them to You and agree for Your Divine blessing over them, their family and the community where they reside, in Jesus' name we pray, together.
Amen.

Loved Ones' Birth Days or Other Requests

____

____

____

____

June 27

Our wonderful Father in Heaven, we bring to You ALL of Your children who were born on June the 27th and we ask for Your blessings in their lives. We ask that they would know Your love and care as well as Your great plans for them. We ask for You to provide for them and their families, for You to put love and forgiveness in their hearts and for You to keep them safe. We give each one of them to You and agree for Your Divine blessing over them, their family and the community where they reside, in Jesus' name we pray, together.

Amen.

Loved Ones' Birth Days or Other Requests

____

____

____

____

June 28

Our wonderful Father in Heaven, we bring to You ALL of Your children who were born on June the 28th and we ask for Your blessings in their lives. We ask that they would know Your love and care as well as Your great plans for them. We ask for You to provide for them and their families, for You to put love and forgiveness in their hearts and for You to keep them safe. We give each one of them to You and agree for Your Divine blessing over them, their family and the community where they reside, in Jesus' name we pray, together.

Amen.

Loved Ones' Birth Days or Other Requests

____

____

____

____

June 29

Our wonderful Father in Heaven, we bring to You ALL of Your children who were born on June the 29th and we ask for Your blessings in their lives. We ask that they would know Your love and care as well as Your great plans for them. We ask for You to provide for them and their families, for You to put love and forgiveness in their hearts and for You to keep them safe. We give each one of them to You and agree for Your Divine blessing over them, their family and the community where they reside, in Jesus' name we pray, together.

Amen.

Loved Ones' Birth Days or Other Requests

____

____

____

____

June 30

Our wonderful Father in Heaven, we bring to You ALL of Your children who were born on June the 30th and we ask for Your blessings in their lives. We ask that they would know Your love and care as well as Your great plans for them. We ask for You to provide for them and their families, for You to put love and forgiveness in their hearts and for You to keep them safe. We give each one of them to You and agree for Your Divine blessing over them, their family and the community where they reside, in Jesus' name we pray, together.
Amen.

Loved Ones' Birth Days or Other Requests

____

____

____

____

July 1

Our wonderful Father in Heaven, we bring to You ALL of Your children who were born on July the 1st and we ask for Your blessings in their lives. We ask that they would know Your love and care as well as Your great plans for them. We ask for You to provide for them and their families, for You to put love and forgiveness in their hearts and for You to keep them safe. We give each one of them to You and agree for Your Divine blessing over them, their family and the community where they reside, in Jesus' name we pray, together.

Amen.

Loved Ones' Birth Days or Other Requests

____

____

____

____

July 2

Our wonderful Father in Heaven, we bring to You ALL of Your children who were born on July the 2nd and we ask for Your blessings in their lives. We ask that they would know Your love and care as well as Your great plans for them. We ask for You to provide for them and their families, for You to put love and forgiveness in their hearts and for You to keep them safe. We give each one of them to You and agree for Your Divine blessing over them, their family and the community where they reside, in Jesus' name we pray, together.
Amen.

Loved Ones' Birth Days or Other Requests

____

____

____

____

July 3

Our wonderful Father in Heaven, we bring to You ALL of Your children who were born on July the 3rd and we ask for Your blessings in their lives. We ask that they would know Your love and care as well as Your great plans for them. We ask for You to provide for them and their families, for You to put love and forgiveness in their hearts and for You to keep them safe. We give each one of them to You and agree for Your Divine blessing over them, their family and the community where they reside, in Jesus' name we pray, together.
Amen.

Loved Ones' Birth Days or Other Requests

____

____

____

____

July 4

Our wonderful Father in Heaven, we bring to You ALL of Your children who were born on July the 4th and we ask for Your blessings in their lives. We ask that they would know Your love and care as well as Your great plans for them. We ask for You to provide for them and their families, for You to put love and forgiveness in their hearts and for You to keep them safe. We give each one of them to You and agree for Your Divine blessing over them, their family and the community where they reside, in Jesus' name we pray, together.
Amen.

Loved Ones' Birth Days or Other Requests

____

____

____

____

July 5

Our wonderful Father in Heaven, we bring to You ALL of Your children who were born on July the 5th and we ask for Your blessings in their lives. We ask that they would know Your love and care as well as Your great plans for them. We ask for You to provide for them and their families, for You to put love and forgiveness in their hearts and for You to keep them safe. We give each one of them to You and agree for Your Divine blessing over them, their family and the community where they reside, in Jesus' name we pray, together.

Amen.

Loved Ones' Birth Days or Other Requests

____

____

____

____

July 6

Our wonderful Father in Heaven, we bring to You ALL of Your children who were born on July the 6th and we ask for Your blessings in their lives. We ask that they would know Your love and care as well as Your great plans for them. We ask for You to provide for them and their families, for You to put love and forgiveness in their hearts and for You to keep them safe. We give each one of them to You and agree for Your Divine blessing over them, their family and the community where they reside, in Jesus' name we pray, together.
Amen.

Loved Ones' Birth Days or Other Requests

____

____

____

____

July 7

Our wonderful Father in Heaven, we bring to You ALL of Your children who were born on July the 7th and we ask for Your blessings in their lives. We ask that they would know Your love and care as well as Your great plans for them. We ask for You to provide for them and their families, for You to put love and forgiveness in their hearts and for You to keep them safe. We give each one of them to You and agree for Your Divine blessing over them, their family and the community where they reside, in Jesus' name we pray, together.

Amen.

Loved Ones' Birth Days or Other Requests

____

____

____

____

July 8

Our wonderful Father in Heaven, we bring to You ALL of Your children who were born on July the 8th and we ask for Your blessings in their lives. We ask that they would know Your love and care as well as Your great plans for them. We ask for You to provide for them and their families, for You to put love and forgiveness in their hearts and for You to keep them safe. We give each one of them to You and agree for Your Divine blessing over them, their family and the community where they reside, in Jesus' name we pray, together.
Amen.

Loved Ones' Birth Days or Other Requests

____

____

____

____

July 9

Our wonderful Father in Heaven, we bring to You ALL of Your children who were born on July the 9th and we ask for Your blessings in their lives. We ask that they would know Your love and care as well as Your great plans for them. We ask for You to provide for them and their families, for You to put love and forgiveness in their hearts and for You to keep them safe. We give each one of them to You and agree for Your Divine blessing over them, their family and the community where they reside, in Jesus' name we pray, together.
Amen.

Loved Ones' Birth Days or Other Requests

____

____

____

____

July 10

Our wonderful Father in Heaven, we bring to You ALL of Your children who were born on July the 10th and we ask for Your blessings in their lives. We ask that they would know Your love and care as well as Your great plans for them. We ask for You to provide for them and their families, for You to put love and forgiveness in their hearts and for You to keep them safe. We give each one of them to You and agree for Your Divine blessing over them, their family and the community where they reside, in Jesus' name we pray, together.

Amen.

Loved Ones' Birth Days or Other Requests

____

____

____

____

July 11

Our wonderful Father in Heaven, we bring to You ALL of Your children who were born on July the 11th and we ask for Your blessings in their lives. We ask that they would know Your love and care as well as Your great plans for them. We ask for You to provide for them and their families, for You to put love and forgiveness in their hearts and for You to keep them safe. We give each one of them to You and agree for Your Divine blessing over them, their family and the community where they reside, in Jesus' name we pray, together.
Amen.

Loved Ones' Birth Days or Other Requests

____

____

____

____

July 12

Our wonderful Father in Heaven, we bring to You ALL of Your children who were born on July the 12th and we ask for Your blessings in their lives. We ask that they would know Your love and care as well as Your great plans for them. We ask for You to provide for them and their families, for You to put love and forgiveness in their hearts and for You to keep them safe. We give each one of them to You and agree for Your Divine blessing over them, their family and the community where they reside, in Jesus' name we pray, together.
Amen.

Loved Ones' Birth Days or Other Requests

____

____

____

____

July 13

Our wonderful Father in Heaven, we bring to You ALL of Your children who were born on July the 13th and we ask for Your blessings in their lives. We ask that they would know Your love and care as well as Your great plans for them. We ask for You to provide for them and their families, for You to put love and forgiveness in their hearts and for You to keep them safe. We give each one of them to You and agree for Your Divine blessing over them, their family and the community where they reside, in Jesus' name we pray, together.
Amen.

Loved Ones' Birth Days or Other Requests

____

____

____

____

July 14

Our wonderful Father in Heaven, we bring to You ALL of Your children who were born on July the 14th and we ask for Your blessings in their lives. We ask that they would know Your love and care as well as Your great plans for them. We ask for You to provide for them and their families, for You to put love and forgiveness in their hearts and for You to keep them safe. We give each one of them to You and agree for Your Divine blessing over them, their family and the community where they reside, in Jesus' name we pray, together.

Amen.

Loved Ones' Birth Days or Other Requests

____

____

____

____

July 15

Our wonderful Father in Heaven, we bring to You ALL of Your children who were born on July the 15th and we ask for Your blessings in their lives. We ask that they would know Your love and care as well as Your great plans for them. We ask for You to provide for them and their families, for You to put love and forgiveness in their hearts and for You to keep them safe. We give each one of them to You and agree for Your Divine blessing over them, their family and the community where they reside, in Jesus' name we pray, together.
Amen.

Loved Ones' Birth Days or Other Requests

____

____

____

____

July 16

Our wonderful Father in Heaven, we bring to You ALL of Your children who were born on July the 16th and we ask for Your blessings in their lives. We ask that they would know Your love and care as well as Your great plans for them. We ask for You to provide for them and their families, for You to put love and forgiveness in their hearts and for You to keep them safe. We give each one of them to You and agree for Your Divine blessing over them, their family and the community where they reside, in Jesus' name we pray, together.
Amen.

Loved Ones' Birth Days or Other Requests

____

____

____

____

July 17

Our wonderful Father in Heaven, we bring to You ALL of Your children who were born on July the 17th and we ask for Your blessings in their lives. We ask that they would know Your love and care as well as Your great plans for them. We ask for You to provide for them and their families, for You to put love and forgiveness in their hearts and for You to keep them safe. We give each one of them to You and agree for Your Divine blessing over them, their family and the community where they reside, in Jesus' name we pray, together.
Amen.

Loved Ones' Birth Days or Other Requests

____

____

____

____

July 18

Our wonderful Father in Heaven, we bring to You ALL of Your children who were born on July the 18th and we ask for Your blessings in their lives. We ask that they would know Your love and care as well as Your great plans for them. We ask for You to provide for them and their families, for You to put love and forgiveness in their hearts and for You to keep them safe. We give each one of them to You and agree for Your Divine blessing over them, their family and the community where they reside, in Jesus' name we pray, together.

Amen.

Loved Ones' Birth Days or Other Requests

____

____

____

____

July 19

Our wonderful Father in Heaven, we bring to You ALL of Your children who were born on July the 19th and we ask for Your blessings in their lives. We ask that they would know Your love and care as well as Your great plans for them. We ask for You to provide for them and their families, for You to put love and forgiveness in their hearts and for You to keep them safe. We give each one of them to You and agree for Your Divine blessing over them, their family and the community where they reside, in Jesus' name we pray, together.
Amen.

Loved Ones' Birth Days or Other Requests

____

____

____

____

July 20

Our wonderful Father in Heaven, we bring to You ALL of Your children who were born on July the 20th and we ask for Your blessings in their lives. We ask that they would know Your love and care as well as Your great plans for them. We ask for You to provide for them and their families, for You to put love and forgiveness in their hearts and for You to keep them safe. We give each one of them to You and agree for Your Divine blessing over them, their family and the community where they reside, in Jesus' name we pray, together.
Amen.

Loved Ones' Birth Days or Other Requests

____

____

____

____

July 21

Our wonderful Father in Heaven, we bring to You ALL of Your children who were born on July the 21st and we ask for Your blessings in their lives. We ask that they would know Your love and care as well as Your great plans for them. We ask for You to provide for them and their families, for You to put love and forgiveness in their hearts and for You to keep them safe. We give each one of them to You and agree for Your Divine blessing over them, their family and the community where they reside, in Jesus' name we pray, together.
Amen.

Loved Ones' Birth Days or Other Requests

____

____

____

____

July 22

Our wonderful Father in Heaven, we bring to You ALL of Your children who were born on July the 22nd and we ask for Your blessings in their lives. We ask that they would know Your love and care as well as Your great plans for them. We ask for You to provide for them and their families, for You to put love and forgiveness in their hearts and for You to keep them safe. We give each one of them to You and agree for Your Divine blessing over them, their family and the community where they reside, in Jesus' name we pray, together.

Amen.

Loved Ones' Birth Days or Other Requests

____

____

____

____

July 23

Our wonderful Father in Heaven, we bring to You ALL of Your children who were born on July the 23rd and we ask for Your blessings in their lives. We ask that they would know Your love and care as well as Your great plans for them. We ask for You to provide for them and their families, for You to put love and forgiveness in their hearts and for You to keep them safe. We give each one of them to You and agree for Your Divine blessing over them, their family and the community where they reside, in Jesus' name we pray, together.
Amen.

Loved Ones' Birth Days or Other Requests

____

____

____

____

July 24

Our wonderful Father in Heaven, we bring to You ALL of Your children who were born on July the 24th and we ask for Your blessings in their lives. We ask that they would know Your love and care as well as Your great plans for them. We ask for You to provide for them and their families, for You to put love and forgiveness in their hearts and for You to keep them safe. We give each one of them to You and agree for Your Divine blessing over them, their family and the community where they reside, in Jesus' name we pray, together.
Amen.

Loved Ones' Birth Days or Other Requests

____

____

____

____

July 25

Our wonderful Father in Heaven, we bring to You ALL of Your children who were born on July the 25th and we ask for Your blessings in their lives. We ask that they would know Your love and care as well as Your great plans for them. We ask for You to provide for them and their families, for You to put love and forgiveness in their hearts and for You to keep them safe. We give each one of them to You and agree for Your Divine blessing over them, their family and the community where they reside, in Jesus' name we pray, together.
Amen.

Loved Ones' Birth Days or Other Requests

____

____

____

____

July 26

Our wonderful Father in Heaven, we bring to You ALL of Your children who were born on July the 26th and we ask for Your blessings in their lives. We ask that they would know Your love and care as well as Your great plans for them. We ask for You to provide for them and their families, for You to put love and forgiveness in their hearts and for You to keep them safe. We give each one of them to You and agree for Your Divine blessing over them, their family and the community where they reside, in Jesus' name we pray, together.

Amen.

Loved Ones' Birth Days or Other Requests

____

____

____

____

July 27

Our wonderful Father in Heaven, we bring to You ALL of Your children who were born on July the 27th and we ask for Your blessings in their lives. We ask that they would know Your love and care as well as Your great plans for them. We ask for You to provide for them and their families, for You to put love and forgiveness in their hearts and for You to keep them safe. We give each one of them to You and agree for Your Divine blessing over them, their family and the community where they reside, in Jesus' name we pray, together.

Amen.

Loved Ones' Birth Days or Other Requests

____

____

____

____

July 28

Our wonderful Father in Heaven, we bring to You ALL of Your children who were born on July the 28th and we ask for Your blessings in their lives. We ask that they would know Your love and care as well as Your great plans for them. We ask for You to provide for them and their families, for You to put love and forgiveness in their hearts and for You to keep them safe. We give each one of them to You and agree for Your Divine blessing over them, their family and the community where they reside, in Jesus' name we pray, together.
Amen.

Loved Ones' Birth Days or Other Requests

____

____

____

____

July 29

Our wonderful Father in Heaven, we bring to You ALL of Your children who were born on July the 29th and we ask for Your blessings in their lives. We ask that they would know Your love and care as well as Your great plans for them. We ask for You to provide for them and their families, for You to put love and forgiveness in their hearts and for You to keep them safe. We give each one of them to You and agree for Your Divine blessing over them, their family and the community where they reside, in Jesus' name we pray, together.
Amen.

Loved Ones' Birth Days or Other Requests

____

____

____

____

July 30

Our wonderful Father in Heaven, we bring to You ALL of Your children who were born on July the 30th and we ask for Your blessings in their lives. We ask that they would know Your love and care as well as Your great plans for them. We ask for You to provide for them and their families, for You to put love and forgiveness in their hearts and for You to keep them safe. We give each one of them to You and agree for Your Divine blessing over them, their family and the community where they reside, in Jesus' name we pray, together.
Amen.

Loved Ones' Birth Days or Other Requests

____

____

____

____

July 31

Our wonderful Father in Heaven, we bring to You ALL of Your children who were born on July the 31st and we ask for Your blessings in their lives. We ask that they would know Your love and care as well as Your great plans for them. We ask for You to provide for them and their families, for You to put love and forgiveness in their hearts and for You to keep them safe. We give each one of them to You and agree for Your Divine blessing over them, their family and the community where they reside, in Jesus' name we pray, together.
Amen.

Loved Ones' Birth Days or Other Requests

____

____

____

____

August 1

Our wonderful Father in Heaven, we bring to You ALL of Your children who were born on August the 1st and we ask for Your blessings in their lives. We ask that they would know Your love and care as well as Your great plans for them. We ask for You to provide for them and their families, for You to put love and forgiveness in their hearts and for You to keep them safe. We give each one of them to You and agree for Your Divine blessing over them, their family and the community where they reside, in Jesus' name we pray, together.

Amen.

Loved Ones' Birth Days or Other Requests

August 2

Our wonderful Father in Heaven, we bring to You ALL of Your children who were born on August the 2nd and we ask for Your blessings in their lives. We ask that they would know Your love and care as well as Your great plans for them. We ask for You to provide for them and their families, for You to put love and forgiveness in their hearts and for You to keep them safe. We give each one of them to You and agree for Your Divine blessing over them, their family and the community where they reside, in Jesus' name we pray, together.
Amen.

Loved Ones' Birth Days or Other Requests

____

____

____

____

August 3

Our wonderful Father in Heaven, we bring to You ALL of Your children who were born on August the 3rd and we ask for Your blessings in their lives. We ask that they would know Your love and care as well as Your great plans for them. We ask for You to provide for them and their families, for You to put love and forgiveness in their hearts and for You to keep them safe. We give each one of them to You and agree for Your Divine blessing over them, their family and the community where they reside, in Jesus' name we pray, together.

Amen.

Loved Ones' Birth Days or Other Requests

____

____

____

____

August 4

Our wonderful Father in Heaven, we bring to You ALL of Your children who were born on August the 4th and we ask for Your blessings in their lives. We ask that they would know Your love and care as well as Your great plans for them. We ask for You to provide for them and their families, for You to put love and forgiveness in their hearts and for You to keep them safe. We give each one of them to You and agree for Your Divine blessing over them, their family and the community where they reside, in Jesus' name we pray, together.

Amen.

Loved Ones' Birth Days or Other Requests

____

____

____

____

August 5

Our wonderful Father in Heaven, we bring to You ALL of Your children who were born on August the 5th and we ask for Your blessings in their lives. We ask that they would know Your love and care as well as Your great plans for them. We ask for You to provide for them and their families, for You to put love and forgiveness in their hearts and for You to keep them safe. We give each one of them to You and agree for Your Divine blessing over them, their family and the community where they reside, in Jesus' name we pray, together.
Amen.

Loved Ones' Birth Days or Other Requests

____

____

____

____

August 6

Our wonderful Father in Heaven, we bring to You ALL of Your children who were born on August the 6th and we ask for Your blessings in their lives. We ask that they would know Your love and care as well as Your great plans for them. We ask for You to provide for them and their families, for You to put love and forgiveness in their hearts and for You to keep them safe. We give each one of them to You and agree for Your Divine blessing over them, their family and the community where they reside, in Jesus' name we pray, together.

Amen.

Loved Ones' Birth Days or Other Requests

____

____

____

____

August 7

Our wonderful Father in Heaven, we bring to You ALL of Your children who were born on August the 7th and we ask for Your blessings in their lives. We ask that they would know Your love and care as well as Your great plans for them. We ask for You to provide for them and their families, for You to put love and forgiveness in their hearts and for You to keep them safe. We give each one of them to You and agree for Your Divine blessing over them, their family and the community where they reside, in Jesus' name we pray, together.
Amen.

Loved Ones' Birth Days or Other Requests

____

____

____

____

August 8

Our wonderful Father in Heaven, we bring to You ALL of Your children who were born on August the 8th and we ask for Your blessings in their lives. We ask that they would know Your love and care as well as Your great plans for them. We ask for You to provide for them and their families, for You to put love and forgiveness in their hearts and for You to keep them safe. We give each one of them to You and agree for Your Divine blessing over them, their family and the community where they reside, in Jesus' name we pray, together.

Amen.

Loved Ones' Birth Days or Other Requests

____

____

____

____

August 9

Our wonderful Father in Heaven, we bring to You ALL of Your children who were born on August the 9th and we ask for Your blessings in their lives. We ask that they would know Your love and care as well as Your great plans for them. We ask for You to provide for them and their families, for You to put love and forgiveness in their hearts and for You to keep them safe. We give each one of them to You and agree for Your Divine blessing over them, their family and the community where they reside, in Jesus' name we pray, together.

Amen.

Loved Ones' Birth Days or Other Requests

____

____

____

____

August 10

Our wonderful Father in Heaven, we bring to You ALL of Your children who were born on August the 10th and we ask for Your blessings in their lives. We ask that they would know Your love and care as well as Your great plans for them. We ask for You to provide for them and their families, for You to put love and forgiveness in their hearts and for You to keep them safe. We give each one of them to You and agree for Your Divine blessing over them, their family and the community where they reside, in Jesus' name we pray, together.

Amen.

Loved Ones' Birth Days or Other Requests

____

____

____

____

August 11

Our wonderful Father in Heaven, we bring to You ALL of Your children who were born on August the 11th and we ask for Your blessings in their lives. We ask that they would know Your love and care as well as Your great plans for them. We ask for You to provide for them and their families, for You to put love and forgiveness in their hearts and for You to keep them safe. We give each one of them to You and agree for Your Divine blessing over them, their family and the community where they reside, in Jesus' name we pray, together.

Amen.

Loved Ones' Birth Days or Other Requests

____

____

____

____

August 12

Our wonderful Father in Heaven, we bring to You ALL of Your children who were born on August the 12th and we ask for Your blessings in their lives. We ask that they would know Your love and care as well as Your great plans for them. We ask for You to provide for them and their families, for You to put love and forgiveness in their hearts and for You to keep them safe. We give each one of them to You and agree for Your Divine blessing over them, their family and the community where they reside, in Jesus' name we pray, together.
Amen.

Loved Ones' Birth Days or Other Requests

____

____

____

____

August 13

Our wonderful Father in Heaven, we bring to You ALL of Your children who were born on August the 13th and we ask for Your blessings in their lives. We ask that they would know Your love and care as well as Your great plans for them. We ask for You to provide for them and their families, for You to put love and forgiveness in their hearts and for You to keep them safe. We give each one of them to You and agree for Your Divine blessing over them, their family and the community where they reside, in Jesus' name we pray, together.

Amen.

Loved Ones' Birth Days or Other Requests

____

____

____

____

August 14

Our wonderful Father in Heaven, we bring to You ALL of Your children who were born on August the 14th and we ask for Your blessings in their lives. We ask that they would know Your love and care as well as Your great plans for them. We ask for You to provide for them and their families, for You to put love and forgiveness in their hearts and for You to keep them safe. We give each one of them to You and agree for Your Divine blessing over them, their family and the community where they reside, in Jesus' name we pray, together.

Amen.

Loved Ones' Birth Days or Other Requests

____

____

____

____

August 15

Our wonderful Father in Heaven, we bring to You ALL of Your children who were born on August the 15th and we ask for Your blessings in their lives. We ask that they would know Your love and care as well as Your great plans for them. We ask for You to provide for them and their families, for You to put love and forgiveness in their hearts and for You to keep them safe. We give each one of them to You and agree for Your Divine blessing over them, their family and the community where they reside, in Jesus' name we pray, together.

Amen.

Loved Ones' Birth Days or Other Requests

____

____

____

____

August 16

Our wonderful Father in Heaven, we bring to You ALL of Your children who were born on August the 16th and we ask for Your blessings in their lives. We ask that they would know Your love and care as well as Your great plans for them. We ask for You to provide for them and their families, for You to put love and forgiveness in their hearts and for You to keep them safe. We give each one of them to You and agree for Your Divine blessing over them, their family and the community where they reside, in Jesus' name we pray, together.

Amen.

Loved Ones' Birth Days or Other Requests

____

____

____

____

August 17

Our wonderful Father in Heaven, we bring to You ALL of Your children who were born on August the 17th and we ask for Your blessings in their lives. We ask that they would know Your love and care as well as Your great plans for them. We ask for You to provide for them and their families, for You to put love and forgiveness in their hearts and for You to keep them safe. We give each one of them to You and agree for Your Divine blessing over them, their family and the community where they reside, in Jesus' name we pray, together.

Amen.

Loved Ones' Birth Days or Other Requests

____

____

____

____

August 18

Our wonderful Father in Heaven, we bring to You ALL of Your children who were born on August the 18th and we ask for Your blessings in their lives. We ask that they would know Your love and care as well as Your great plans for them. We ask for You to provide for them and their families, for You to put love and forgiveness in their hearts and for You to keep them safe. We give each one of them to You and agree for Your Divine blessing over them, their family and the community where they reside, in Jesus' name we pray, together.

Amen.

Loved Ones' Birth Days or Other Requests

____

____

____

____

August 19

Our wonderful Father in Heaven, we bring to You ALL of Your children who were born on August the 19th and we ask for Your blessings in their lives. We ask that they would know Your love and care as well as Your great plans for them. We ask for You to provide for them and their families, for You to put love and forgiveness in their hearts and for You to keep them safe. We give each one of them to You and agree for Your Divine blessing over them, their family and the community where they reside, in Jesus' name we pray, together.

Amen.

Loved Ones' Birth Days or Other Requests

____

____

____

____

August 20

Our wonderful Father in Heaven, we bring to You ALL of Your children who were born on August the 20th and we ask for Your blessings in their lives. We ask that they would know Your love and care as well as Your great plans for them. We ask for You to provide for them and their families, for You to put love and forgiveness in their hearts and for You to keep them safe. We give each one of them to You and agree for Your Divine blessing over them, their family and the community where they reside, in Jesus' name we pray, together.

Amen.

Loved Ones' Birth Days or Other Requests

____

____

____

____

August 21

Our wonderful Father in Heaven, we bring to You ALL of Your children who were born on August the 21st and we ask for Your blessings in their lives. We ask that they would know Your love and care as well as Your great plans for them. We ask for You to provide for them and their families, for You to put love and forgiveness in their hearts and for You to keep them safe. We give each one of them to You and agree for Your Divine blessing over them, their family and the community where they reside, in Jesus' name we pray, together.
Amen.

Loved Ones' Birth Days or Other Requests

____

____

____

____

August 22

Our wonderful Father in Heaven, we bring to You ALL of Your children who were born on August the 22nd and we ask for Your blessings in their lives. We ask that they would know Your love and care as well as Your great plans for them. We ask for You to provide for them and their families, for You to put love and forgiveness in their hearts and for You to keep them safe. We give each one of them to You and agree for Your Divine blessing over them, their family and the community where they reside, in Jesus' name we pray, together.
Amen.

Loved Ones' Birth Days or Other Requests

____

____

____

____

August 23

Our wonderful Father in Heaven, we bring to You ALL of Your children who were born on August the 23rd and we ask for Your blessings in their lives. We ask that they would know Your love and care as well as Your great plans for them. We ask for You to provide for them and their families, for You to put love and forgiveness in their hearts and for You to keep them safe. We give each one of them to You and agree for Your Divine blessing over them, their family and the community where they reside, in Jesus' name we pray, together.
Amen.

Loved Ones' Birth Days or Other Requests

____

____

____

____

August 24

Our wonderful Father in Heaven, we bring to You ALL of Your children who were born on August the 24th and we ask for Your blessings in their lives. We ask that they would know Your love and care as well as Your great plans for them. We ask for You to provide for them and their families, for You to put love and forgiveness in their hearts and for You to keep them safe. We give each one of them to You and agree for Your Divine blessing over them, their family and the community where they reside, in Jesus' name we pray, together.
Amen.

Loved Ones' Birth Days or Other Requests

____

____

____

____

August 25

Our wonderful Father in Heaven, we bring to You ALL of Your children who were born on August the 25th and we ask for Your blessings in their lives. We ask that they would know Your love and care as well as Your great plans for them. We ask for You to provide for them and their families, for You to put love and forgiveness in their hearts and for You to keep them safe. We give each one of them to You and agree for Your Divine blessing over them, their family and the community where they reside, in Jesus' name we pray, together.
Amen.

Loved Ones' Birth Days or Other Requests

____

____

____

____

August 26

Our wonderful Father in Heaven, we bring to You ALL of Your children who were born on August the 26th and we ask for Your blessings in their lives. We ask that they would know Your love and care as well as Your great plans for them. We ask for You to provide for them and their families, for You to put love and forgiveness in their hearts and for You to keep them safe. We give each one of them to You and agree for Your Divine blessing over them, their family and the community where they reside, in Jesus' name we pray, together.
Amen.

Loved Ones' Birth Days or Other Requests

____

____

____

____

August 27

Our wonderful Father in Heaven, we bring to You ALL of Your children who were born on August the 27th and we ask for Your blessings in their lives. We ask that they would know Your love and care as well as Your great plans for them. We ask for You to provide for them and their families, for You to put love and forgiveness in their hearts and for You to keep them safe. We give each one of them to You and agree for Your Divine blessing over them, their family and the community where they reside, in Jesus' name we pray, together.

Amen.

Loved Ones' Birth Days or Other Requests

____

____

____

____

August 28

Our wonderful Father in Heaven, we bring to You ALL of Your children who were born on August the 28th and we ask for Your blessings in their lives. We ask that they would know Your love and care as well as Your great plans for them. We ask for You to provide for them and their families, for You to put love and forgiveness in their hearts and for You to keep them safe. We give each one of them to You and agree for Your Divine blessing over them, their family and the community where they reside, in Jesus' name we pray, together.
Amen.

Loved Ones' Birth Days or Other Requests

____

____

____

____

August 29

Our wonderful Father in Heaven, we bring to You ALL of Your children who were born on August the 29th and we ask for Your blessings in their lives. We ask that they would know Your love and care as well as Your great plans for them. We ask for You to provide for them and their families, for You to put love and forgiveness in their hearts and for You to keep them safe. We give each one of them to You and agree for Your Divine blessing over them, their family and the community where they reside, in Jesus' name we pray, together.

Amen.

Loved Ones' Birth Days or Other Requests

____

____

____

____

August 30

Our wonderful Father in Heaven, we bring to You ALL of Your children who were born on August the 30th and we ask for Your blessings in their lives. We ask that they would know Your love and care as well as Your great plans for them. We ask for You to provide for them and their families, for You to put love and forgiveness in their hearts and for You to keep them safe. We give each one of them to You and agree for Your Divine blessing over them, their family and the community where they reside, in Jesus' name we pray, together.

Amen.

Loved Ones' Birth Days or Other Requests

____

____

____

____

August 31

Our wonderful Father in Heaven, we bring to You ALL of Your children who were born on August the 31st and we ask for Your blessings in their lives. We ask that they would know Your love and care as well as Your great plans for them. We ask for You to provide for them and their families, for You to put love and forgiveness in their hearts and for You to keep them safe. We give each one of them to You and agree for Your Divine blessing over them, their family and the community where they reside, in Jesus' name we pray, together.
Amen.

Loved Ones' Birth Days or Other Requests

____

____

____

____

September 1

Our wonderful Father in Heaven, we bring to You ALL of Your children who were born on September the 1st and we ask for Your blessings in their lives. We ask that they would know Your love and care as well as Your great plans for them. We ask for You to provide for them and their families, for You to put love and forgiveness in their hearts and for You to keep them safe. We give each one of them to You and agree for Your Divine blessing over them, their family and the community where they reside, in Jesus' name we pray, together.
Amen.

Loved Ones' Birth Days or Other Requests

____

____

____

____

September 2

Our wonderful Father in Heaven, we bring to You ALL of Your children who were born on September the 2nd and we ask for Your blessings in their lives. We ask that they would know Your love and care as well as Your great plans for them. We ask for You to provide for them and their families, for You to put love and forgiveness in their hearts and for You to keep them safe. We give each one of them to You and agree for Your Divine blessing over them, their family and the community where they reside, in Jesus' name we pray, together.

Amen.

Loved Ones' Birth Days or Other Requests

____

____

____

____

September 3

Our wonderful Father in Heaven, we bring to You ALL of Your children who were born on September the 3rd and we ask for Your blessings in their lives. We ask that they would know Your love and care as well as Your great plans for them. We ask for You to provide for them and their families, for You to put love and forgiveness in their hearts and for You to keep them safe. We give each one of them to You and agree for Your Divine blessing over them, their family and the community where they reside, in Jesus' name we pray, together.

Amen.

Loved Ones' Birth Days or Other Requests

____

____

____

____

September 4

Our wonderful Father in Heaven, we bring to You ALL of Your children who were born on September the 4th and we ask for Your blessings in their lives. We ask that they would know Your love and care as well as Your great plans for them. We ask for You to provide for them and their families, for You to put love and forgiveness in their hearts and for You to keep them safe. We give each one of them to You and agree for Your Divine blessing over them, their family and the community where they reside, in Jesus' name we pray, together.

Amen.

Loved Ones' Birth Days or Other Requests

____

____

____

____

September 5

Our wonderful Father in Heaven, we bring to You ALL of Your children who were born on September the 5th and we ask for Your blessings in their lives. We ask that they would know Your love and care as well as Your great plans for them. We ask for You to provide for them and their families, for You to put love and forgiveness in their hearts and for You to keep them safe. We give each one of them to You and agree for Your Divine blessing over them, their family and the community where they reside, in Jesus' name we pray, together.
Amen.

Loved Ones' Birth Days or Other Requests

____

____

____

____

September 6

Our wonderful Father in Heaven, we bring to You ALL of Your children who were born on September the 6th and we ask for Your blessings in their lives. We ask that they would know Your love and care as well as Your great plans for them. We ask for You to provide for them and their families, for You to put love and forgiveness in their hearts and for You to keep them safe. We give each one of them to You and agree for Your Divine blessing over them, their family and the community where they reside, in Jesus' name we pray, together.
Amen.

Loved Ones' Birth Days or Other Requests

____

____

____

____

September 7

Our wonderful Father in Heaven, we bring to You ALL of Your children who were born on September the 7th and we ask for Your blessings in their lives. We ask that they would know Your love and care as well as Your great plans for them. We ask for You to provide for them and their families, for You to put love and forgiveness in their hearts and for You to keep them safe. We give each one of them to You and agree for Your Divine blessing over them, their family and the community where they reside, in Jesus' name we pray, together.

Amen.

Loved Ones' Birth Days or Other Requests

____

____

____

____

September 8

Our wonderful Father in Heaven, we bring to You ALL of Your children who were born on September the 8th and we ask for Your blessings in their lives. We ask that they would know Your love and care as well as Your great plans for them. We ask for You to provide for them and their families, for You to put love and forgiveness in their hearts and for You to keep them safe. We give each one of them to You and agree for Your Divine blessing over them, their family and the community where they reside, in Jesus' name we pray, together.
Amen.

Loved Ones' Birth Days or Other Requests

____

____

____

____

September 9

Our wonderful Father in Heaven, we bring to You ALL of Your children who were born on September the 9th and we ask for Your blessings in their lives. We ask that they would know Your love and care as well as Your great plans for them. We ask for You to provide for them and their families, for You to put love and forgiveness in their hearts and for You to keep them safe. We give each one of them to You and agree for Your Divine blessing over them, their family and the community where they reside, in Jesus' name we pray, together.

Amen.

Loved Ones' Birth Days or Other Requests

____

____

____

____

September 10

Our wonderful Father in Heaven, we bring to You ALL of Your children who were born on September the 10th and we ask for Your blessings in their lives. We ask that they would know Your love and care as well as Your great plans for them. We ask for You to provide for them and their families, for You to put love and forgiveness in their hearts and for You to keep them safe. We give each one of them to You and agree for Your Divine blessing over them, their family and the community where they reside, in Jesus' name we pray, together.

Amen.

Loved Ones' Birth Days or Other Requests

____

____

____

____

September 11

Our wonderful Father in Heaven, we bring to You ALL of Your children who were born on September the 11th and we ask for Your blessings in their lives. We ask that they would know Your love and care as well as Your great plans for them. We ask for You to provide for them and their families, for You to put love and forgiveness in their hearts and for You to keep them safe. We give each one of them to You and agree for Your Divine blessing over them, their family and the community where they reside, in Jesus' name we pray, together.

Amen.

Loved Ones' Birth Days or Other Requests

____

____

____

____

September 12

Our wonderful Father in Heaven, we bring to You ALL of Your children who were born on September the 12th and we ask for Your blessings in their lives. We ask that they would know Your love and care as well as Your great plans for them. We ask for You to provide for them and their families, for You to put love and forgiveness in their hearts and for You to keep them safe. We give each one of them to You and agree for Your Divine blessing over them, their family and the community where they reside, in Jesus' name we pray, together.
Amen.

Loved Ones' Birth Days or Other Requests

____

____

____

____

September 13

Our wonderful Father in Heaven, we bring to You ALL of Your children who were born on September the 13th and we ask for Your blessings in their lives. We ask that they would know Your love and care as well as Your great plans for them. We ask for You to provide for them and their families, for You to put love and forgiveness in their hearts and for You to keep them safe. We give each one of them to You and agree for Your Divine blessing over them, their family and the community where they reside, in Jesus' name we pray, together.
Amen.

Loved Ones' Birth Days or Other Requests

____

____

____

____

September 14

Our wonderful Father in Heaven, we bring to You ALL of Your children who were born on September the 14th and we ask for Your blessings in their lives. We ask that they would know Your love and care as well as Your great plans for them. We ask for You to provide for them and their families, for You to put love and forgiveness in their hearts and for You to keep them safe. We give each one of them to You and agree for Your Divine blessing over them, their family and the community where they reside, in Jesus' name we pray, together.
Amen.

Loved Ones' Birth Days or Other Requests

____

____

____

____

September 15

Our wonderful Father in Heaven, we bring to You ALL of Your children who were born on September the 15th and we ask for Your blessings in their lives. We ask that they would know Your love and care as well as Your great plans for them. We ask for You to provide for them and their families, for You to put love and forgiveness in their hearts and for You to keep them safe. We give each one of them to You and agree for Your Divine blessing over them, their family and the community where they reside, in Jesus' name we pray, together.

Amen.

Loved Ones' Birth Days or Other Requests

____

____

____

____

September 16

Our wonderful Father in Heaven, we bring to You ALL of Your children who were born on September the 16th and we ask for Your blessings in their lives. We ask that they would know Your love and care as well as Your great plans for them. We ask for You to provide for them and their families, for You to put love and forgiveness in their hearts and for You to keep them safe. We give each one of them to You and agree for Your Divine blessing over them, their family and the community where they reside, in Jesus' name we pray, together.
Amen.

Loved Ones' Birth Days or Other Requests

____

____

____

____

September 17

Our wonderful Father in Heaven, we bring to You ALL of Your children who were born on September the 17th and we ask for Your blessings in their lives. We ask that they would know Your love and care as well as Your great plans for them. We ask for You to provide for them and their families, for You to put love and forgiveness in their hearts and for You to keep them safe. We give each one of them to You and agree for Your Divine blessing over them, their family and the community where they reside, in Jesus' name we pray, together.
Amen.

Loved Ones' Birth Days or Other Requests

____

____

____

____

September 18

Our wonderful Father in Heaven, we bring to You ALL of Your children who were born on September the 18th and we ask for Your blessings in their lives. We ask that they would know Your love and care as well as Your great plans for them. We ask for You to provide for them and their families, for You to put love and forgiveness in their hearts and for You to keep them safe. We give each one of them to You and agree for Your Divine blessing over them, their family and the community where they reside, in Jesus' name we pray, together.
Amen.

Loved Ones' Birth Days or Other Requests

____

____

____

____

September 19

Our wonderful Father in Heaven, we bring to You ALL of Your children who were born on September the 19th and we ask for Your blessings in their lives. We ask that they would know Your love and care as well as Your great plans for them. We ask for You to provide for them and their families, for You to put love and forgiveness in their hearts and for You to keep them safe. We give each one of them to You and agree for Your Divine blessing over them, their family and the community where they reside, in Jesus' name we pray, together.

Amen.

Loved Ones' Birth Days or Other Requests

____

____

____

____

September 21

Our wonderful Father in Heaven, we bring to You ALL of Your children who were born on September the 21st and we ask for Your blessings in their lives. We ask that they would know Your love and care as well as Your great plans for them. We ask for You to provide for them and their families, for You to put love and forgiveness in their hearts and for You to keep them safe. We give each one of them to You and agree for Your Divine blessing over them, their family and the community where they reside, in Jesus' name we pray, together.
Amen.

Loved Ones' Birth Days or Other Requests

____

____

____

____

September 20

Our wonderful Father in Heaven, we bring to You ALL of Your children who were born on September the 20th and we ask for Your blessings in their lives. We ask that they would know Your love and care as well as Your great plans for them. We ask for You to provide for them and their families, for You to put love and forgiveness in their hearts and for You to keep them safe. We give each one of them to You and agree for Your Divine blessing over them, their family and the community where they reside, in Jesus' name we pray, together.
Amen.

Loved Ones' Birth Days or Other Requests

September 22

Our wonderful Father in Heaven, we bring to You ALL of Your children who were born on September the 22nd and we ask for Your blessings in their lives. We ask that they would know Your love and care as well as Your great plans for them. We ask for You to provide for them and their families, for You to put love and forgiveness in their hearts and for You to keep them safe. We give each one of them to You and agree for Your Divine blessing over them, their family and the community where they reside, in Jesus' name we pray, together.
Amen.

Loved Ones' Birth Days or Other Requests

____

____

____

____

September 23

Our wonderful Father in Heaven, we bring to You ALL of Your children who were born on September the 23rd and we ask for Your blessings in their lives. We ask that they would know Your love and care as well as Your great plans for them. We ask for You to provide for them and their families, for You to put love and forgiveness in their hearts and for You to keep them safe. We give each one of them to You and agree for Your Divine blessing over them, their family and the community where they reside, in Jesus' name we pray, together.

Amen.

Loved Ones' Birth Days or Other Requests

____

____

____

____

September 24

Our wonderful Father in Heaven, we bring to You ALL of Your children who were born on September the 24th and we ask for Your blessings in their lives. We ask that they would know Your love and care as well as Your great plans for them. We ask for You to provide for them and their families, for You to put love and forgiveness in their hearts and for You to keep them safe. We give each one of them to You and agree for Your Divine blessing over them, their family and the community where they reside, in Jesus' name we pray, together.
Amen.

Loved Ones' Birth Days or Other Requests

____

____

____

____

September 25

Our wonderful Father in Heaven, we bring to You ALL of Your children who were born on September the 25th and we ask for Your blessings in their lives. We ask that they would know Your love and care as well as Your great plans for them. We ask for You to provide for them and their families, for You to put love and forgiveness in their hearts and for You to keep them safe. We give each one of them to You and agree for Your Divine blessing over them, their family and the community where they reside, in Jesus' name we pray, together.

Amen.

Loved Ones' Birth Days or Other Requests

____

____

____

____

September 26

Our wonderful Father in Heaven, we bring to You ALL of Your children who were born on September the 26th and we ask for Your blessings in their lives. We ask that they would know Your love and care as well as Your great plans for them. We ask for You to provide for them and their families, for You to put love and forgiveness in their hearts and for You to keep them safe. We give each one of them to You and agree for Your Divine blessing over them, their family and the community where they reside, in Jesus' name we pray, together.
Amen.

Loved Ones' Birth Days or Other Requests

____

____

____

____

September 27

Our wonderful Father in Heaven, we bring to You ALL of Your children who were born on September the 27th and we ask for Your blessings in their lives. We ask that they would know Your love and care as well as Your great plans for them. We ask for You to provide for them and their families, for You to put love and forgiveness in their hearts and for You to keep them safe. We give each one of them to You and agree for Your Divine blessing over them, their family and the community where they reside, in Jesus' name we pray, together.
Amen.

Loved Ones' Birth Days or Other Requests

____

____

____

____

September 28

Our wonderful Father in Heaven, we bring to You ALL of Your children who were born on September the 28th and we ask for Your blessings in their lives. We ask that they would know Your love and care as well as Your great plans for them. We ask for You to provide for them and their families, for You to put love and forgiveness in their hearts and for You to keep them safe. We give each one of them to You and agree for Your Divine blessing over them, their family and the community where they reside, in Jesus' name we pray, together.
Amen.

Loved Ones' Birth Days or Other Requests

____

____

____

____

September 29

Our wonderful Father in Heaven, we bring to You ALL of Your children who were born on September the 29th and we ask for Your blessings in their lives. We ask that they would know Your love and care as well as Your great plans for them. We ask for You to provide for them and their families, for You to put love and forgiveness in their hearts and for You to keep them safe. We give each one of them to You and agree for Your Divine blessing over them, their family and the community where they reside, in Jesus' name we pray, together.

Amen.

Loved Ones' Birth Days or Other Requests

____

____

____

____

September 30

Our wonderful Father in Heaven, we bring to You ALL of Your children who were born on September the 30th and we ask for Your blessings in their lives. We ask that they would know Your love and care as well as Your great plans for them. We ask for You to provide for them and their families, for You to put love and forgiveness in their hearts and for You to keep them safe. We give each one of them to You and agree for Your Divine blessing over them, their family and the community where they reside, in Jesus' name we pray, together.

Amen.

Loved Ones' Birth Days or Other Requests

____

____

____

____

October 1

Our wonderful Father in Heaven, we bring to You ALL of Your children who were born on October the 1st and we ask for Your blessings in their lives. We ask that they would know Your love and care as well as Your great plans for them. We ask for You to provide for them and their families, for You to put love and forgiveness in their hearts and for You to keep them safe. We give each one of them to You and agree for Your Divine blessing over them, their family and the community where they reside, in Jesus' name we pray, together.
Amen.

Loved Ones' Birth Days or Other Requests

____

____

____

____

October 2

Our wonderful Father in Heaven, we bring to You ALL of Your children who were born on October the 2nd and we ask for Your blessings in their lives. We ask that they would know Your love and care as well as Your great plans for them. We ask for You to provide for them and their families, for You to put love and forgiveness in their hearts and for You to keep them safe. We give each one of them to You and agree for Your Divine blessing over them, their family and the community where they reside, in Jesus' name we pray, together.
Amen.

Loved Ones' Birth Days or Other Requests

____

____

____

____

October 3

Our wonderful Father in Heaven, we bring to You ALL of Your children who were born on October the 3rd and we ask for Your blessings in their lives. We ask that they would know Your love and care as well as Your great plans for them. We ask for You to provide for them and their families, for You to put love and forgiveness in their hearts and for You to keep them safe. We give each one of them to You and agree for Your Divine blessing over them, their family and the community where they reside, in Jesus' name we pray, together.
Amen.

Loved Ones' Birth Days or Other Requests

____

____

____

____

October 4

Our wonderful Father in Heaven, we bring to You ALL of Your children who were born on October the 4th and we ask for Your blessings in their lives. We ask that they would know Your love and care as well as Your great plans for them. We ask for You to provide for them and their families, for You to put love and forgiveness in their hearts and for You to keep them safe. We give each one of them to You and agree for Your Divine blessing over them, their family and the community where they reside, in Jesus' name we pray, together.
Amen.

Loved Ones' Birth Days or Other Requests

____

____

____

____

October 5

Our wonderful Father in Heaven, we bring to You ALL of Your children who were born on October the 5th and we ask for Your blessings in their lives. We ask that they would know Your love and care as well as Your great plans for them. We ask for You to provide for them and their families, for You to put love and forgiveness in their hearts and for You to keep them safe. We give each one of them to You and agree for Your Divine blessing over them, their family and the community where they reside, in Jesus' name we pray, together.
Amen.

Loved Ones' Birth Days or Other Requests

____

____

____

____

October 6

Our wonderful Father in Heaven, we bring to You ALL of Your children who were born on October the 6th and we ask for Your blessings in their lives. We ask that they would know Your love and care as well as Your great plans for them. We ask for You to provide for them and their families, for You to put love and forgiveness in their hearts and for You to keep them safe. We give each one of them to You and agree for Your Divine blessing over them, their family and the community where they reside, in Jesus' name we pray, together.
Amen.

Loved Ones' Birth Days or Other Requests

____

____

____

____

October 7

Our wonderful Father in Heaven, we bring to You ALL of Your children who were born on October the 7th and we ask for Your blessings in their lives. We ask that they would know Your love and care as well as Your great plans for them. We ask for You to provide for them and their families, for You to put love and forgiveness in their hearts and for You to keep them safe. We give each one of them to You and agree for Your Divine blessing over them, their family and the community where they reside, in Jesus' name we pray, together.
Amen.

Loved Ones' Birth Days or Other Requests

____

____

____

____

October 8

Our wonderful Father in Heaven, we bring to You ALL of Your children who were born on October the 8th and we ask for Your blessings in their lives. We ask that they would know Your love and care as well as Your great plans for them. We ask for You to provide for them and their families, for You to put love and forgiveness in their hearts and for You to keep them safe. We give each one of them to You and agree for Your Divine blessing over them, their family and the community where they reside, in Jesus' name we pray, together.
Amen.

Loved Ones' Birth Days or Other Requests

____

____

____

____

October 9

Our wonderful Father in Heaven, we bring to You ALL of Your children who were born on October the 9th and we ask for Your blessings in their lives. We ask that they would know Your love and care as well as Your great plans for them. We ask for You to provide for them and their families, for You to put love and forgiveness in their hearts and for You to keep them safe. We give each one of them to You and agree for Your Divine blessing over them, their family and the community where they reside, in Jesus' name we pray, together.

Amen.

Loved Ones' Birth Days or Other Requests

____

____

____

____

October 10

Our wonderful Father in Heaven, we bring to You ALL of Your children who were born on October the 10th and we ask for Your blessings in their lives. We ask that they would know Your love and care as well as Your great plans for them. We ask for You to provide for them and their families, for You to put love and forgiveness in their hearts and for You to keep them safe. We give each one of them to You and agree for Your Divine blessing over them, their family and the community where they reside, in Jesus' name we pray, together.

Amen.

Loved Ones' Birth Days or Other Requests

____

____

____

____

October 11

Our wonderful Father in Heaven, we bring to You ALL of Your children who were born on October the 11th and we ask for Your blessings in their lives. We ask that they would know Your love and care as well as Your great plans for them. We ask for You to provide for them and their families, for You to put love and forgiveness in their hearts and for You to keep them safe. We give each one of them to You and agree for Your Divine blessing over them, their family and the community where they reside, in Jesus' name we pray, together.

Amen.

Loved Ones' Birth Days or Other Requests

____

____

____

____

October 12

Our wonderful Father in Heaven, we bring to You ALL of Your children who were born on October the 12th and we ask for Your blessings in their lives. We ask that they would know Your love and care as well as Your great plans for them. We ask for You to provide for them and their families, for You to put love and forgiveness in their hearts and for You to keep them safe. We give each one of them to You and agree for Your Divine blessing over them, their family and the community where they reside, in Jesus' name we pray, together.
Amen.

Loved Ones' Birth Days or Other Requests

____

____

____

____

October 13

Our wonderful Father in Heaven, we bring to You ALL of Your children who were born on October the 13th and we ask for Your blessings in their lives. We ask that they would know Your love and care as well as Your great plans for them. We ask for You to provide for them and their families, for You to put love and forgiveness in their hearts and for You to keep them safe. We give each one of them to You and agree for Your Divine blessing over them, their family and the community where they reside, in Jesus' name we pray, together.

Amen.

Loved Ones' Birth Days or Other Requests

____

____

____

____

October 14

Our wonderful Father in Heaven, we bring to You ALL of Your children who were born on October the 14th and we ask for Your blessings in their lives. We ask that they would know Your love and care as well as Your great plans for them. We ask for You to provide for them and their families, for You to put love and forgiveness in their hearts and for You to keep them safe. We give each one of them to You and agree for Your Divine blessing over them, their family and the community where they reside, in Jesus' name we pray, together.
Amen.

Loved Ones' Birth Days or Other Requests

____

____

____

____

October 15

Our wonderful Father in Heaven, we bring to You ALL of Your children who were born on October the 15th and we ask for Your blessings in their lives. We ask that they would know Your love and care as well as Your great plans for them. We ask for You to provide for them and their families, for You to put love and forgiveness in their hearts and for You to keep them safe. We give each one of them to You and agree for Your Divine blessing over them, their family and the community where they reside, in Jesus' name we pray, together.

Amen.

Loved Ones' Birth Days or Other Requests

____

____

____

____

October 16

Our wonderful Father in Heaven, we bring to You ALL of Your children who were born on October the 16th and we ask for Your blessings in their lives. We ask that they would know Your love and care as well as Your great plans for them. We ask for You to provide for them and their families, for You to put love and forgiveness in their hearts and for You to keep them safe. We give each one of them to You and agree for Your Divine blessing over them, their family and the community where they reside, in Jesus' name we pray, together.

Amen.

Loved Ones' Birth Days or Other Requests

____

____

____

____

October 17

Our wonderful Father in Heaven, we bring to You ALL of Your children who were born on October the 17th and we ask for Your blessings in their lives. We ask that they would know Your love and care as well as Your great plans for them. We ask for You to provide for them and their families, for You to put love and forgiveness in their hearts and for You to keep them safe. We give each one of them to You and agree for Your Divine blessing over them, their family and the community where they reside, in Jesus' name we pray, together.

Amen.

Loved Ones' Birth Days or Other Requests

____

____

____

____

October 18

Our wonderful Father in Heaven, we bring to You ALL of Your children who were born on October the 18th and we ask for Your blessings in their lives. We ask that they would know Your love and care as well as Your great plans for them. We ask for You to provide for them and their families, for You to put love and forgiveness in their hearts and for You to keep them safe. We give each one of them to You and agree for Your Divine blessing over them, their family and the community where they reside, in Jesus' name we pray, together.

Amen.

Loved Ones' Birth Days or Other Requests

____

____

____

____

October 19

Our wonderful Father in Heaven, we bring to You ALL of Your children who were born on October the 19th and we ask for Your blessings in their lives. We ask that they would know Your love and care as well as Your great plans for them. We ask for You to provide for them and their families, for You to put love and forgiveness in their hearts and for You to keep them safe. We give each one of them to You and agree for Your Divine blessing over them, their family and the community where they reside, in Jesus' name we pray, together.
Amen.

Loved Ones' Birth Days or Other Requests

____

____

____

____

October 20

Our wonderful Father in Heaven, we bring to You ALL of Your children who were born on October the 20th and we ask for Your blessings in their lives. We ask that they would know Your love and care as well as Your great plans for them. We ask for You to provide for them and their families, for You to put love and forgiveness in their hearts and for You to keep them safe. We give each one of them to You and agree for Your Divine blessing over them, their family and the community where they reside, in Jesus' name we pray, together.

Amen.

Loved Ones' Birth Days or Other Requests

____

____

____

____

October 21

Our wonderful Father in Heaven, we bring to You ALL of Your children who were born on October the 21st and we ask for Your blessings in their lives. We ask that they would know Your love and care as well as Your great plans for them. We ask for You to provide for them and their families, for You to put love and forgiveness in their hearts and for You to keep them safe. We give each one of them to You and agree for Your Divine blessing over them, their family and the community where they reside, in Jesus' name we pray, together.

Amen.

Loved Ones' Birth Days or Other Requests

____

____

____

____

October 22

Our wonderful Father in Heaven, we bring to You ALL of Your children who were born on October the 22nd and we ask for Your blessings in their lives. We ask that they would know Your love and care as well as Your great plans for them. We ask for You to provide for them and their families, for You to put love and forgiveness in their hearts and for You to keep them safe. We give each one of them to You and agree for Your Divine blessing over them, their family and the community where they reside, in Jesus' name we pray, together.

Amen.

Loved Ones' Birth Days or Other Requests

____

____

____

____

October 23

Our wonderful Father in Heaven, we bring to You ALL of Your children who were born on October the 23rd and we ask for Your blessings in their lives. We ask that they would know Your love and care as well as Your great plans for them. We ask for You to provide for them and their families, for You to put love and forgiveness in their hearts and for You to keep them safe. We give each one of them to You and agree for Your Divine blessing over them, their family and the community where they reside, in Jesus' name we pray, together.
Amen.

Loved Ones' Birth Days or Other Requests

____

____

____

____

October 24

Our wonderful Father in Heaven, we bring to You ALL of Your children who were born on October the 24th and we ask for Your blessings in their lives. We ask that they would know Your love and care as well as Your great plans for them. We ask for You to provide for them and their families, for You to put love and forgiveness in their hearts and for You to keep them safe. We give each one of them to You and agree for Your Divine blessing over them, their family and the community where they reside, in Jesus' name we pray, together.

Amen.

Loved Ones' Birth Days or Other Requests

____

____

____

____

October 25

Our wonderful Father in Heaven, we bring to You ALL of Your children who were born on October the 25th and we ask for Your blessings in their lives. We ask that they would know Your love and care as well as Your great plans for them. We ask for You to provide for them and their families, for You to put love and forgiveness in their hearts and for You to keep them safe. We give each one of them to You and agree for Your Divine blessing over them, their family and the community where they reside, in Jesus' name we pray, together.
Amen.

Loved Ones' Birth Days or Other Requests

____

____

____

____

October 26

Our wonderful Father in Heaven, we bring to You ALL of Your children who were born on October the 26th and we ask for Your blessings in their lives. We ask that they would know Your love and care as well as Your great plans for them. We ask for You to provide for them and their families, for You to put love and forgiveness in their hearts and for You to keep them safe. We give each one of them to You and agree for Your Divine blessing over them, their family and the community where they reside, in Jesus' name we pray, together.
Amen.

Loved Ones' Birth Days or Other Requests

____

____

____

____

October 27

Our wonderful Father in Heaven, we bring to You ALL of Your children who were born on October the 27th and we ask for Your blessings in their lives. We ask that they would know Your love and care as well as Your great plans for them. We ask for You to provide for them and their families, for You to put love and forgiveness in their hearts and for You to keep them safe. We give each one of them to You and agree for Your Divine blessing over them, their family and the community where they reside, in Jesus' name we pray, together.

Amen.

Loved Ones' Birth Days or Other Requests

____

____

____

____

October 28

Our wonderful Father in Heaven, we bring to You ALL of Your children who were born on October the 28th and we ask for Your blessings in their lives. We ask that they would know Your love and care as well as Your great plans for them. We ask for You to provide for them and their families, for You to put love and forgiveness in their hearts and for You to keep them safe. We give each one of them to You and agree for Your Divine blessing over them, their family and the community where they reside, in Jesus' name we pray, together.

Amen.

Loved Ones' Birth Days or Other Requests

____

____

____

____

October 29

Our wonderful Father in Heaven, we bring to You ALL of Your children who were born on October the 29th and we ask for Your blessings in their lives. We ask that they would know Your love and care as well as Your great plans for them. We ask for You to provide for them and their families, for You to put love and forgiveness in their hearts and for You to keep them safe. We give each one of them to You and agree for Your Divine blessing over them, their family and the community where they reside, in Jesus' name we pray, together.

Amen.

Loved Ones' Birth Days or Other Requests

____

____

____

____

October 30

Our wonderful Father in Heaven, we bring to You ALL of Your children who were born on October the 30th and we ask for Your blessings in their lives. We ask that they would know Your love and care as well as Your great plans for them. We ask for You to provide for them and their families, for You to put love and forgiveness in their hearts and for You to keep them safe. We give each one of them to You and agree for Your Divine blessing over them, their family and the community where they reside, in Jesus' name we pray, together.

Amen.

Loved Ones' Birth Days or Other Requests

____

____

____

____

October 31

Our wonderful Father in Heaven, we bring to You ALL of Your children who were born on October the 31st and we ask for Your blessings in their lives. We ask that they would know Your love and care as well as Your great plans for them. We ask for You to provide for them and their families, for You to put love and forgiveness in their hearts and for You to keep them safe. We give each one of them to You and agree for Your Divine blessing over them, their family and the community where they reside, in Jesus' name we pray, together.
Amen.

Loved Ones' Birth Days or Other Requests

____

____

____

____

November 1

Our wonderful Father in Heaven, we bring to You ALL of Your children who were born on November the 1st and we ask for Your blessings in their lives. We ask that they would know Your love and care as well as Your great plans for them. We ask for You to provide for them and their families, for You to put love and forgiveness in their hearts and for You to keep them safe. We give each one of them to You and agree for Your Divine blessing over them, their family and the community where they reside, in Jesus' name we pray, together.

Amen.

Loved Ones' Birth Days or Other Requests

____

____

____

____

November 2

Our wonderful Father in Heaven, we bring to You ALL of Your children who were born on November the 2nd and we ask for Your blessings in their lives. We ask that they would know Your love and care as well as Your great plans for them. We ask for You to provide for them and their families, for You to put love and forgiveness in their hearts and for You to keep them safe. We give each one of them to You and agree for Your Divine blessing over them, their family and the community where they reside, in Jesus' name we pray, together.

Amen.

Loved Ones' Birth Days or Other Requests

____

____

____

____

November 3

Our wonderful Father in Heaven, we bring to You ALL of Your children who were born on November the 3rd and we ask for Your blessings in their lives. We ask that they would know Your love and care as well as Your great plans for them. We ask for You to provide for them and their families, for You to put love and forgiveness in their hearts and for You to keep them safe. We give each one of them to You and agree for Your Divine blessing over them, their family and the community where they reside, in Jesus' name we pray, together.

Amen.

Loved Ones' Birth Days or Other Requests

____

____

____

____

November 4

Our wonderful Father in Heaven, we bring to You ALL of Your children who were born on November the 4th and we ask for Your blessings in their lives. We ask that they would know Your love and care as well as Your great plans for them. We ask for You to provide for them and their families, for You to put love and forgiveness in their hearts and for You to keep them safe. We give each one of them to You and agree for Your Divine blessing over them, their family and the community where they reside, in Jesus' name we pray, together.

Amen.

Loved Ones' Birth Days or Other Requests

____

____

____

____

November 5

Our wonderful Father in Heaven, we bring to You ALL of Your children who were born on November the 5th and we ask for Your blessings in their lives. We ask that they would know Your love and care as well as Your great plans for them. We ask for You to provide for them and their families, for You to put love and forgiveness in their hearts and for You to keep them safe. We give each one of them to You and agree for Your Divine blessing over them, their family and the community where they reside, in Jesus' name we pray, together.
Amen.

Loved Ones' Birth Days or Other Requests

____

____

____

____

November 6

Our wonderful Father in Heaven, we bring to You ALL of Your children who were born on November the 6th and we ask for Your blessings in their lives. We ask that they would know Your love and care as well as Your great plans for them. We ask for You to provide for them and their families, for You to put love and forgiveness in their hearts and for You to keep them safe. We give each one of them to You and agree for Your Divine blessing over them, their family and the community where they reside, in Jesus' name we pray, together.

Amen.

Loved Ones' Birth Days or Other Requests

____

____

____

____

November 7

Our wonderful Father in Heaven, we bring to You ALL of Your children who were born on November the 7th and we ask for Your blessings in their lives. We ask that they would know Your love and care as well as Your great plans for them. We ask for You to provide for them and their families, for You to put love and forgiveness in their hearts and for You to keep them safe. We give each one of them to You and agree for Your Divine blessing over them, their family and the community where they reside, in Jesus' name we pray, together.

Amen.

Loved Ones' Birth Days or Other Requests

____

____

____

____

November 8

Our wonderful Father in Heaven, we bring to You ALL of Your children who were born on November the 8th and we ask for Your blessings in their lives. We ask that they would know Your love and care as well as Your great plans for them. We ask for You to provide for them and their families, for You to put love and forgiveness in their hearts and for You to keep them safe. We give each one of them to You and agree for Your Divine blessing over them, their family and the community where they reside, in Jesus' name we pray, together.
Amen.

Loved Ones' Birth Days or Other Requests

____

____

____

____

November 9

Our wonderful Father in Heaven, we bring to You ALL of Your children who were born on November the 9th and we ask for Your blessings in their lives. We ask that they would know Your love and care as well as Your great plans for them. We ask for You to provide for them and their families, for You to put love and forgiveness in their hearts and for You to keep them safe. We give each one of them to You and agree for Your Divine blessing over them, their family and the community where they reside, in Jesus' name we pray, together.
Amen.

Loved Ones' Birth Days or Other Requests

____

____

____

____

November 10

Our wonderful Father in Heaven, we bring to You ALL of Your children who were born on November the 10th and we ask for Your blessings in their lives. We ask that they would know Your love and care as well as Your great plans for them. We ask for You to provide for them and their families, for You to put love and forgiveness in their hearts and for You to keep them safe. We give each one of them to You and agree for Your Divine blessing over them, their family and the community where they reside, in Jesus' name we pray, together.
Amen.

Loved Ones' Birth Days or Other Requests

____

____

____

____

November 11

Our wonderful Father in Heaven, we bring to You ALL of Your children who were born on November the 11th and we ask for Your blessings in their lives. We ask that they would know Your love and care as well as Your great plans for them. We ask for You to provide for them and their families, for You to put love and forgiveness in their hearts and for You to keep them safe. We give each one of them to You and agree for Your Divine blessing over them, their family and the community where they reside, in Jesus' name we pray, together.
Amen.

Loved Ones' Birth Days or Other Requests

____

____

____

____

November 12

Our wonderful Father in Heaven, we bring to You ALL of Your children who were born on November the 12th and we ask for Your blessings in their lives. We ask that they would know Your love and care as well as Your great plans for them. We ask for You to provide for them and their families, for You to put love and forgiveness in their hearts and for You to keep them safe. We give each one of them to You and agree for Your Divine blessing over them, their family and the community where they reside, in Jesus' name we pray, together.
Amen.

Loved Ones' Birth Days or Other Requests

____

____

____

____

November 13

Our wonderful Father in Heaven, we bring to You ALL of Your children who were born on November the 13th and we ask for Your blessings in their lives. We ask that they would know Your love and care as well as Your great plans for them. We ask for You to provide for them and their families, for You to put love and forgiveness in their hearts and for You to keep them safe. We give each one of them to You and agree for Your Divine blessing over them, their family and the community where they reside, in Jesus' name we pray, together.
Amen.

Loved Ones' Birth Days or Other Requests

____

____

____

____

November 14

Our wonderful Father in Heaven, we bring to You ALL of Your children who were born on November the 14th and we ask for Your blessings in their lives. We ask that they would know Your love and care as well as Your great plans for them. We ask for You to provide for them and their families, for You to put love and forgiveness in their hearts and for You to keep them safe. We give each one of them to You and agree for Your Divine blessing over them, their family and the community where they reside, in Jesus' name we pray, together.
Amen.

Loved Ones' Birth Days or Other Requests

____

____

____

____

November 15

Our wonderful Father in Heaven, we bring to You ALL of Your children who were born on November the 15th and we ask for Your blessings in their lives. We ask that they would know Your love and care as well as Your great plans for them. We ask for You to provide for them and their families, for You to put love and forgiveness in their hearts and for You to keep them safe. We give each one of them to You and agree for Your Divine blessing over them, their family and the community where they reside, in Jesus' name we pray, together.

Amen.

Loved Ones' Birth Days or Other Requests

____

____

____

____

November 16

Our wonderful Father in Heaven, we bring to You ALL of Your children who were born on November the 16th and we ask for Your blessings in their lives. We ask that they would know Your love and care as well as Your great plans for them. We ask for You to provide for them and their families, for You to put love and forgiveness in their hearts and for You to keep them safe. We give each one of them to You and agree for Your Divine blessing over them, their family and the community where they reside, in Jesus' name we pray, together.

Amen.

Loved Ones' Birth Days or Other Requests

____

____

____

____

November 17

Our wonderful Father in Heaven, we bring to You ALL of Your children who were born on November the 17th and we ask for Your blessings in their lives. We ask that they would know Your love and care as well as Your great plans for them. We ask for You to provide for them and their families, for You to put love and forgiveness in their hearts and for You to keep them safe. We give each one of them to You and agree for Your Divine blessing over them, their family and the community where they reside, in Jesus' name we pray, together.
Amen.

Loved Ones' Birth Days or Other Requests

____

____

____

____

November 18

Our wonderful Father in Heaven, we bring to You ALL of Your children who were born on November the 18th and we ask for Your blessings in their lives. We ask that they would know Your love and care as well as Your great plans for them. We ask for You to provide for them and their families, for You to put love and forgiveness in their hearts and for You to keep them safe. We give each one of them to You and agree for Your Divine blessing over them, their family and the community where they reside, in Jesus' name we pray, together.

Amen.

Loved Ones' Birth Days or Other Requests

____

____

____

____

November 19

Our wonderful Father in Heaven, we bring to You ALL of Your children who were born on November the 19th and we ask for Your blessings in their lives. We ask that they would know Your love and care as well as Your great plans for them. We ask for You to provide for them and their families, for You to put love and forgiveness in their hearts and for You to keep them safe. We give each one of them to You and agree for Your Divine blessing over them, their family and the community where they reside, in Jesus' name we pray, together.
Amen.

Loved Ones' Birth Days or Other Requests

____

____

____

____

November 20

Our wonderful Father in Heaven, we bring to You ALL of Your children who were born on November the 20th and we ask for Your blessings in their lives. We ask that they would know Your love and care as well as Your great plans for them. We ask for You to provide for them and their families, for You to put love and forgiveness in their hearts and for You to keep them safe. We give each one of them to You and agree for Your Divine blessing over them, their family and the community where they reside, in Jesus' name we pray, together.
Amen.

Loved Ones' Birth Days or Other Requests

____

____

____

____

November 21

Our wonderful Father in Heaven, we bring to You ALL of Your children who were born on November the 21st and we ask for Your blessings in their lives. We ask that they would know Your love and care as well as Your great plans for them. We ask for You to provide for them and their families, for You to put love and forgiveness in their hearts and for You to keep them safe. We give each one of them to You and agree for Your Divine blessing over them, their family and the community where they reside, in Jesus' name we pray, together.
Amen.

Loved Ones' Birth Days or Other Requests

____

____

____

____

November 22

Our wonderful Father in Heaven, we bring to You ALL of Your children who were born on November the 22nd and we ask for Your blessings in their lives. We ask that they would know Your love and care as well as Your great plans for them. We ask for You to provide for them and their families, for You to put love and forgiveness in their hearts and for You to keep them safe. We give each one of them to You and agree for Your Divine blessing over them, their family and the community where they reside, in Jesus' name we pray, together.
Amen.

Loved Ones' Birth Days or Other Requests

____

____

____

____

November 23

Our wonderful Father in Heaven, we bring to You ALL of Your children who were born on November the 23rd and we ask for Your blessings in their lives. We ask that they would know Your love and care as well as Your great plans for them. We ask for You to provide for them and their families, for You to put love and forgiveness in their hearts and for You to keep them safe. We give each one of them to You and agree for Your Divine blessing over them, their family and the community where they reside, in Jesus' name we pray, together.
Amen.

Loved Ones' Birth Days or Other Requests

___

___

___

___

November 24

Our wonderful Father in Heaven, we bring to You ALL of Your children who were born on November the 24th and we ask for Your blessings in their lives. We ask that they would know Your love and care as well as Your great plans for them. We ask for You to provide for them and their families, for You to put love and forgiveness in their hearts and for You to keep them safe. We give each one of them to You and agree for Your Divine blessing over them, their family and the community where they reside, in Jesus' name we pray, together.
Amen.

Loved Ones' Birth Days or Other Requests

____

____

____

____

November 25

Our wonderful Father in Heaven, we bring to You ALL of Your children who were born on November the 25th and we ask for Your blessings in their lives. We ask that they would know Your love and care as well as Your great plans for them. We ask for You to provide for them and their families, for You to put love and forgiveness in their hearts and for You to keep them safe. We give each one of them to You and agree for Your Divine blessing over them, their family and the community where they reside, in Jesus' name we pray, together.

Amen.

Loved Ones' Birth Days or Other Requests

____

____

____

____

November 26

Our wonderful Father in Heaven, we bring to You ALL of Your children who were born on November the 26th and we ask for Your blessings in their lives. We ask that they would know Your love and care as well as Your great plans for them. We ask for You to provide for them and their families, for You to put love and forgiveness in their hearts and for You to keep them safe. We give each one of them to You and agree for Your Divine blessing over them, their family and the community where they reside, in Jesus' name we pray, together.

Amen.

Loved Ones' Birth Days or Other Requests

____

____

____

____

November 27

Our wonderful Father in Heaven, we bring to You ALL of Your children who were born on November the 27th and we ask for Your blessings in their lives. We ask that they would know Your love and care as well as Your great plans for them. We ask for You to provide for them and their families, for You to put love and forgiveness in their hearts and for You to keep them safe. We give each one of them to You and agree for Your Divine blessing over them, their family and the community where they reside, in Jesus' name we pray, together.

Amen.

Loved Ones' Birth Days or Other Requests

____

____

____

____

November 28

Our wonderful Father in Heaven, we bring to You ALL of Your children who were born on November the 28th and we ask for Your blessings in their lives. We ask that they would know Your love and care as well as Your great plans for them. We ask for You to provide for them and their families, for You to put love and forgiveness in their hearts and for You to keep them safe. We give each one of them to You and agree for Your Divine blessing over them, their family and the community where they reside, in Jesus' name we pray, together.
Amen.

Loved Ones' Birth Days or Other Requests

____

____

____

____

November 29

Our wonderful Father in Heaven, we bring to You ALL of Your children who were born on November 29th and we ask for Your blessings in their lives. We ask that they would know Your love and care as well as Your great plans for them. We ask for You to provide for them and their families, for You to put love and forgiveness in their hearts and for You to keep them safe. We give each one of them to You and agree for Your Divine blessing over them, their family and the community where they reside, in Jesus' name we pray, together.

Amen.

Loved Ones' Birth Days or Other Requests

____

____

____

____

November 30

Our wonderful Father in Heaven, we bring to You ALL of Your children who were born on November the 30th and we ask for Your blessings in their lives. We ask that they would know Your love and care as well as Your great plans for them. We ask for You to provide for them and their families, for You to put love and forgiveness in their hearts and for You to keep them safe. We give each one of them to You and agree for Your Divine blessing over them, their family and the community where they reside, in Jesus' name we pray, together.
Amen.

Loved Ones' Birth Days or Other Requests

____

____

____

____

December 1

Our wonderful Father in Heaven, we bring to You ALL of Your children who were born on December the 1st and we ask for Your blessings in their lives. We ask that they would know Your love and care as well as Your great plans for them. We ask for You to provide for them and their families, for You to put love and forgiveness in their hearts and for You to keep them safe. We give each one of them to You and agree for Your Divine blessing over them, their family and the community where they reside, in Jesus' name we pray, together.

Amen.

Loved Ones' Birth Days or Other Requests

____

____

____

____

December 2

Our wonderful Father in Heaven, we bring to You ALL of Your children who were born on December the 2nd and we ask for Your blessings in their lives. We ask that they would know Your love and care as well as Your great plans for them. We ask for You to provide for them and their families, for You to put love and forgiveness in their hearts and for You to keep them safe. We give each one of them to You and agree for Your Divine blessing over them, their family and the community where they reside, in Jesus' name we pray, together.

Amen.

Loved Ones' Birth Days or Other Requests

____

____

____

____

December 3

Our wonderful Father in Heaven, we bring to You ALL of Your children who were born on December the 3rd and we ask for Your blessings in their lives. We ask that they would know Your love and care as well as Your great plans for them. We ask for You to provide for them and their families, for You to put love and forgiveness in their hearts and for You to keep them safe. We give each one of them to You and agree for Your Divine blessing over them, their family and the community where they reside, in Jesus' name we pray, together.

Amen.

Loved Ones' Birth Days or Other Requests

____

____

____

____

December 4

Our wonderful Father in Heaven, we bring to You ALL of Your children who were born on December the 4th and we ask for Your blessings in their lives. We ask that they would know Your love and care as well as Your great plans for them. We ask for You to provide for them and their families, for You to put love and forgiveness in their hearts and for You to keep them safe. We give each one of them to You and agree for Your Divine blessing over them, their family and the community where they reside, in Jesus' name we pray, together.
Amen.

Loved Ones' Birth Days or Other Requests

____

____

____

____

December 5

Our wonderful Father in Heaven, we bring to You ALL of Your children who were born on December the 5th and we ask for Your blessings in their lives. We ask that they would know Your love and care as well as Your great plans for them. We ask for You to provide for them and their families, for You to put love and forgiveness in their hearts and for You to keep them safe. We give each one of them to You and agree for Your Divine blessing over them, their family and the community where they reside, in Jesus' name we pray, together.

Amen.

Loved Ones' Birth Days or Other Requests

____

____

____

____

December 6

Our wonderful Father in Heaven, we bring to You ALL of Your children who were born on December the 6th and we ask for Your blessings in their lives. We ask that they would know Your love and care as well as Your great plans for them. We ask for You to provide for them and their families, for You to put love and forgiveness in their hearts and for You to keep them safe. We give each one of them to You and agree for Your Divine blessing over them, their family and the community where they reside, in Jesus' name we pray, together.

Amen.

Loved Ones' Birth Days or Other Requests

____

____

____

____

December 7

Our wonderful Father in Heaven, we bring to You ALL of Your children who were born on December the 7th and we ask for Your blessings in their lives. We ask that they would know Your love and care as well as Your great plans for them. We ask for You to provide for them and their families, for You to put love and forgiveness in their hearts and for You to keep them safe. We give each one of them to You and agree for Your Divine blessing over them, their family and the community where they reside, in Jesus' name we pray, together.
Amen.

Loved Ones' Birth Days or Other Requests

____

____

____

____

December 8

Our wonderful Father in Heaven, we bring to You ALL of Your children who were born on December the 8th and we ask for Your blessings in their lives. We ask that they would know Your love and care as well as Your great plans for them. We ask for You to provide for them and their families, for You to put love and forgiveness in their hearts and for You to keep them safe. We give each one of them to You and agree for Your Divine blessing over them, their family and the community where they reside, in Jesus' name we pray, together.
Amen.

Loved Ones' Birth Days or Other Requests

____

____

____

____

December 9

Our wonderful Father in Heaven, we bring to You ALL of Your children who were born on December the 9th and we ask for Your blessings in their lives. We ask that they would know Your love and care as well as Your great plans for them. We ask for You to provide for them and their families, for You to put love and forgiveness in their hearts and for You to keep them safe. We give each one of them to You and agree for Your Divine blessing over them, their family and the community where they reside, in Jesus' name we pray, together.

Amen.

Loved Ones' Birth Days or Other Requests

____

____

____

____

December 10

Our wonderful Father in Heaven, we bring to You ALL of Your children who were born on December the 10th and we ask for Your blessings in their lives. We ask that they would know Your love and care as well as Your great plans for them. We ask for You to provide for them and their families, for You to put love and forgiveness in their hearts and for You to keep them safe. We give each one of them to You and agree for Your Divine blessing over them, their family and the community where they reside, in Jesus' name we pray, together.
Amen.

Loved Ones' Birth Days or Other Requests

____

____

____

____

December 11

Our wonderful Father in Heaven, we bring to You ALL of Your children who were born on December the 11th and we ask for Your blessings in their lives. We ask that they would know Your love and care as well as Your great plans for them. We ask for You to provide for them and their families, for You to put love and forgiveness in their hearts and for You to keep them safe. We give each one of them to You and agree for Your Divine blessing over them, their family and the community where they reside, in Jesus' name we pray, together.

Amen.

Loved Ones' Birth Days or Other Requests

____

____

____

____

December 12

Our wonderful Father in Heaven, we bring to You ALL of Your children who were born on December the 12th and we ask for Your blessings in their lives. We ask that they would know Your love and care as well as Your great plans for them. We ask for You to provide for them and their families, for You to put love and forgiveness in their hearts and for You to keep them safe. We give each one of them to You and agree for Your Divine blessing over them, their family and the community where they reside, in Jesus' name we pray, together.
Amen.

Loved Ones' Birth Days or Other Requests

____

____

____

____

December 13

Our wonderful Father in Heaven, we bring to You ALL of Your children who were born on December the 13th and we ask for Your blessings in their lives. We ask that they would know Your love and care as well as Your great plans for them. We ask for You to provide for them and their families, for You to put love and forgiveness in their hearts and for You to keep them safe. We give each one of them to You and agree for Your Divine blessing over them, their family and the community where they reside, in Jesus' name we pray, together.
Amen.

Loved Ones' Birth Days or Other Requests

____

____

____

____

December 14

Our wonderful Father in Heaven, we bring to You ALL of Your children who were born on December the 14th and we ask for Your blessings in their lives. We ask that they would know Your love and care as well as Your great plans for them. We ask for You to provide for them and their families, for You to put love and forgiveness in their hearts and for You to keep them safe. We give each one of them to You and agree for Your Divine blessing over them, their family and the community where they reside, in Jesus' name we pray, together.
Amen.

Loved Ones' Birth Days or Other Requests

____

____

____

____

December 15

Our wonderful Father in Heaven, we bring to You ALL of Your children who were born on December the 15th and we ask for Your blessings in their lives. We ask that they would know Your love and care as well as Your great plans for them. We ask for You to provide for them and their families, for You to put love and forgiveness in their hearts and for You to keep them safe. We give each one of them to You and agree for Your Divine blessing over them, their family and the community where they reside, in Jesus' name we pray, together.

Amen.

Loved Ones' Birth Days or Other Requests

____

____

____

____

December 16

Our wonderful Father in Heaven, we bring to You ALL of Your children who were born on December the 16th and we ask for Your blessings in their lives. We ask that they would know Your love and care as well as Your great plans for them. We ask for You to provide for them and their families, for You to put love and forgiveness in their hearts and for You to keep them safe. We give each one of them to You and agree for Your Divine blessing over them, their family and the community where they reside, in Jesus' name we pray, together.
Amen.

Loved Ones' Birth Days or Other Requests

____

____

____

____

December 17

Our wonderful Father in Heaven, we bring to You ALL of Your children who were born on December the 17th and we ask for Your blessings in their lives. We ask that they would know Your love and care as well as Your great plans for them. We ask for You to provide for them and their families, for You to put love and forgiveness in their hearts and for You to keep them safe. We give each one of them to You and agree for Your Divine blessing over them, their family and the community where they reside, in Jesus' name we pray, together.

Amen.

Loved Ones' Birth Days or Other Requests

____

____

____

____

December 18

Our wonderful Father in Heaven, we bring to You ALL of Your children who were born on December the 18th and we ask for Your blessings in their lives. We ask that they would know Your love and care as well as Your great plans for them. We ask for You to provide for them and their families, for You to put love and forgiveness in their hearts and for You to keep them safe. We give each one of them to You and agree for Your Divine blessing over them, their family and the community where they reside, in Jesus' name we pray, together.

Amen.

Loved Ones' Birth Days or Other Requests

____

____

____

____

December 19

Our wonderful Father in Heaven, we bring to You ALL of Your children who were born on December the 19th and we ask for Your blessings in their lives. We ask that they would know Your love and care as well as Your great plans for them. We ask for You to provide for them and their families, for You to put love and forgiveness in their hearts and for You to keep them safe. We give each one of them to You and agree for Your Divine blessing over them, their family and the community where they reside, in Jesus' name we pray, together.

Amen.

Loved Ones' Birth Days or Other Requests

____

____

____

____

December 20

Our wonderful Father in Heaven, we bring to You ALL of Your children who were born on December the 20th and we ask for Your blessings in their lives. We ask that they would know Your love and care as well as Your great plans for them. We ask for You to provide for them and their families, for You to put love and forgiveness in their hearts and for You to keep them safe. We give each one of them to You and agree for Your Divine blessing over them, their family and the community where they reside, in Jesus' name we pray, together.
Amen.

Loved Ones' Birth Days or Other Requests

____

____

____

____

December 21

Our wonderful Father in Heaven, we bring to You ALL of Your children who were born on December the 21st and we ask for Your blessings in their lives. We ask that they would know Your love and care as well as Your great plans for them. We ask for You to provide for them and their families, for You to put love and forgiveness in their hearts and for You to keep them safe. We give each one of them to You and agree for Your Divine blessing over them, their family and the community where they reside, in Jesus' name we pray, together.

Amen.

Loved Ones' Birth Days or Other Requests

____

____

____

____

December 22

Our wonderful Father in Heaven, we bring to You ALL of Your children who were born on December the 22nd and we ask for Your blessings in their lives. We ask that they would know Your love and care as well as Your great plans for them. We ask for You to provide for them and their families, for You to put love and forgiveness in their hearts and for You to keep them safe. We give each one of them to You and agree for Your Divine blessing over them, their family and the community where they reside, in Jesus' name we pray, together.

Amen.

Loved Ones' Birth Days or Other Requests

____

____

____

____

December 23

Our wonderful Father in Heaven, we bring to You ALL of Your children who were born on December the 23rd and we ask for Your blessings in their lives. We ask that they would know Your love and care as well as Your great plans for them. We ask for You to provide for them and their families, for You to put love and forgiveness in their hearts and for You to keep them safe. We give each one of them to You and agree for Your Divine blessing over them, their family and the community where they reside, in Jesus' name we pray, together.
Amen.

Loved Ones' Birth Days or Other Requests

____

____

____

____

December 24

Our wonderful Father in Heaven, we bring to You ALL of Your children who were born on December the 24th and we ask for Your blessings in their lives. We ask that they would know Your love and care as well as Your great plans for them. We ask for You to provide for them and their families, for You to put love and forgiveness in their hearts and for You to keep them safe. We give each one of them to You and agree for Your Divine blessing over them, their family and the community where they reside, in Jesus' name we pray, together.
Amen.

Loved Ones' Birth Days or Other Requests

____

____

____

____

December 25

Our wonderful Father in Heaven, we bring to You ALL of Your children who were born on December the 25th and we ask for Your blessings in their lives. We ask that they would know Your love and care as well as Your great plans for them. We ask for You to provide for them and their families, for You to put love and forgiveness in their hearts and for You to keep them safe. We give each one of them to You and agree for Your Divine blessing over them, their family and the community where they reside, in Jesus' name we pray, together.

Amen.

Loved Ones' Birth Days or Other Requests

____

____

____

____

December 26

Our wonderful Father in Heaven, we bring to You ALL of Your children who were born on December the 26th and we ask for Your blessings in their lives. We ask that they would know Your love and care as well as Your great plans for them. We ask for You to provide for them and their families, for You to put love and forgiveness in their hearts and for You to keep them safe. We give each one of them to You and agree for Your Divine blessing over them, their family and the community where they reside, in Jesus' name we pray, together.

Amen.

Loved Ones' Birth Days or Other Requests

____

____

____

____

December 27

Our wonderful Father in Heaven, we bring to You ALL of Your children who were born on December the 27th and we ask for Your blessings in their lives. We ask that they would know Your love and care as well as Your great plans for them. We ask for You to provide for them and their families, for You to put love and forgiveness in their hearts and for You to keep them safe. We give each one of them to You and agree for Your Divine blessing over them, their family and the community where they reside, in Jesus' name we pray, together.

Amen.

Loved Ones' Birth Days or Other Requests

____

____

____

____

December 28

Our wonderful Father in Heaven, we bring to You ALL of Your children who were born on December the 28th and we ask for Your blessings in their lives. We ask that they would know Your love and care as well as Your great plans for them. We ask for You to provide for them and their families, for You to put love and forgiveness in their hearts and for You to keep them safe. We give each one of them to You and agree for Your Divine blessing over them, their family and the community where they reside, in Jesus' name we pray, together.

Amen.

Loved Ones' Birth Days or Other Requests

____

____

____

____

December 29

Our wonderful Father in Heaven, we bring to You ALL of Your children who were born on December the 29th and we ask for Your blessings in their lives. We ask that they would know Your love and care as well as Your great plans for them. We ask for You to provide for them and their families, for You to put love and forgiveness in their hearts and for You to keep them safe. We give each one of them to You and agree for Your Divine blessing over them, their family and the community where they reside, in Jesus' name we pray, together.
Amen.

Loved Ones' Birth Days or Other Requests

____

____

____

____

December 30

Our wonderful Father in Heaven, we bring to You ALL of Your children who were born on December the 30th and we ask for Your blessings in their lives. We ask that they would know Your love and care as well as Your great plans for them. We ask for You to provide for them and their families, for You to put love and forgiveness in their hearts and for You to keep them safe. We give each one of them to You and agree for Your Divine blessing over them, their family and the community where they reside, in Jesus' name we pray, together.
Amen.

Loved Ones' Birth Days or Other Requests

____

____

____

____

December 31

Our wonderful Father in Heaven, we bring to You ALL of Your children who were born on December the 31st and we ask for Your blessings in their lives. We ask that they would know Your love and care as well as Your great plans for them. We ask for You to provide for them and their families, for You to put love and forgiveness in their hearts and for You to keep them safe. We give each one of them to You and agree for Your Divine blessing over them, their family and the community where they reside, in Jesus' name we pray, together.
Amen.

Loved Ones' Birth Days or Other Requests

____

____

____

____

Made in the USA
Columbia, SC
27 May 2024

35893871R00221